Living Whole

Redefining Singlehood with Power, Passion, and Purpose

Titilope Lawal

©2025

Copyright © 2025 Titilope Lawal

All rights reserved.

No part of this publication may be reproduced, distributed, or transmitted in any form or by any means, including photocopying, recording, or other electronic or mechanical methods, without the prior written permission of the author or publisher, except in the case of brief quotations embodied in critical reviews and certain other noncommercial uses permitted by copyright law.

ISBNS: Paperback: 978-1-7644236-0-1

Hardcover: 978-1-7644236-1-8

Table of Contents

Introduction 8

Chapter 1 12

Embracing God's Divine Identity: Your Worth Beyond Relationship Status 12

    Understanding Your Divine DNA: Created for Purpose 15

    Breaking Free from Society's Definition of Worth 17

    Cultivating Unshakeable Identity in Christ 19

Chapter 2 23

Breaking Free: Overcoming Cultural Myths About Singleness 23

    Identifying and Challenging Cultural Myths: Understanding Common Misconceptions About Singleness 25

        Myth #1: To Be Single Is to Be Lonely 25

        Myth #2: You're Single Because Something Is Wrong with You 26

        Myth #3: All Singles Must Be Desperately Searching 26

        Myth #4: A Partner Is Necessary for Wholeness 27

        Myth #5: A Single Life Lacks Meaning 27

        Myth #6: You Are "Behind" in Life 28

    Redefining Singlehood: God's Perspective on Singleness and Purpose 29

Chapter 3 33

Cultivating Wholeness: The Journey to Self-Discovery and Purpose . 33

    Understanding Biblical Wholeness: Complete in Christ 35

    Aligning Your Daily Life with Divine Purpose: Creating a Vision for Your Life 40

Chapter 4 46

Sacred Solitude: Finding Joy in the Present Season 46

    The Divine Purpose of Solitude: Understanding God's Purpose in Alone Seasons 48

    From Loneliness to Wholeness: Transforming Quiet Moments into Joy 50

    Creating Sacred Spaces: Practical Steps for Meaningful Solitude .. 53

Chapter 5 58

Building Your Life: Career, Calling, and Purpose 58

    Discerning Your Divine Purpose: Understanding the Difference Between Career and Calling 60

    Strategic Career Building: Aligning Professional Goals with Kingdom Purpose 64

    Creating Impact Beyond the Workplace: Developing a Life of Meaningful Service 67

Chapter 6 74

Boundaries and Blessings: Navigating Family and Social Expectations 74

Setting Biblical Boundaries Without Guilt: Understanding God's Design for Healthy Relationships 76

Managing Family Dynamics: Balancing Honor with Personal Space 79

Responding to Social Pressure: Maintaining Grace Under Scrutiny 81

Chapter 7 86

Financial Freedom: Creating Stability and Success as a Single 86

Biblical Stewardship: Understanding God's Principles for Financial Management 88

Strategic Wealth Building: Investment Strategies and Long-term Planning for Singles 90

Biblical Wisdom for Wealth Building 93

Essential Components of Emergency Readiness 94

Success Mindset 95

Chapter 8 99

Community and Connection: Building Meaningful Relationships 99

Building Bonds That Last 100

Creating Spaces for Authentic Connection 100

Cultivating Deep Friendships: Moving Beyond Surface-Level Connections 102

Building a Support System: The Power of Intentional Community 105

Maintaining Healthy Boundaries: Balancing Independence and Interdependence 107

Chapter 9 114

Healing and Hope: Processing Past Relationships with Grace 114

    Embracing God's Healing Grace: Moving from Hurt to Wholeness 116

    Rewriting Your Relationship Narrative: Finding Purpose in Past Pain 118

    Building Healthy Boundaries: Protecting Your Heart While Remaining Open 120

Chapter 10 126

Knowing Yourself in God: Building Your Inner Home 126

    Laying the Foundation: Your Core Values 127

    Learning the Wiring: Your Emotional Patterns 127

    Decorating the Rooms with Grace: Embracing Your Story 128

    Seeing Yourself Through God's Eyes 128

Chapter 11 132

Purpose Over Pressure: Living Beyond Expectations 132

    Your Purpose Is Not Postponed 133

    The Poison of Comparison 134

    When Purpose Feels Delayed 134

    Living from Purpose, Not for Pressure 135

Chapter 12 138

Living Without Limits: Thriving in Your Single Season 138

Breaking Free from Self-Limiting Beliefs: Embracing Your Full Potential 140

Creating a Legacy: Making an Impact Beyond Relationship Status 143

Taking Bold Steps: Practical Strategies for Pursuing Your Purpose 145

Conclusion 149

Acknowledgement 151

REFERENCE 154

Introduction

In many cultures, there's an unspoken pressure that treats being single as a problem that must be fixed. People act as if singleness is a pause in life — a waiting period before "real" living begins. You're told, directly or indirectly, that time is running out and you must hurry to find someone before it's too late. This is so widespread that it puts many single people under pressure and threat. They may fall into depression and isolation, feeling inadequate, unwanted or broken and perceive that there is something wrong with them because no one finds them attractive. Meanwhile, those who are married or in relationships are often seen as more successful or complete. This sneaks into everyday discussions as often as possible: "Are you not going to settle down?" "When should we come to your celebration?" "When is the bell going to ring?" "Whose turn is it next?" These questions, though common, reinforce the idea that being single is a failure — that everyone must find a partner, no matter who, just to fit in. But singleness is not a curse or a consequence of being unmarried, nor is it a blank page of life before love begins. It's a valid and valuable part of life. The belief that one's happiness or worth depends on another person is deeply harmful. True joy and fulfillment come from within, not from the presence of someone else. What if we reverse the narrative and view this period as a time to understand ourselves, cultivate a meaningful life, and explore our gifts and talents rather than wallowing in the sadness of being single, seeing it as a blessing rather than a burden?

Redefining singleness as a season of thoughtful achievements, rather than a sentence, can transform it into a time for growth, authenticity, understanding one's identity, and inclusiveness, loving oneself, being loved, showing love, making a positive impact, and finding fulfillment. Whether you decide to be single for a season or a lifetime, celebrate that season and do not mourn it. "It's a full, vibrant, meaningful chapter of its own."

But what if your life wasn't waiting to begin with marriage?

What if your singlehood was already holy, purposeful, and powerful because God designed it that way?

This book is written for you to understand singlehood through God's eyes. To understand that it's not a life on hold. It's not second-best. It's a sacred season, and for some, a lifelong calling. And for the duration of time you are single, it is not a mistake because purpose is never postponed by relationship status.

Have you ever paused to truly see yourself not through society's expectations or cultural demands, but through the divine lens of your God? In a world that often measures worth by relationship status, we're embarking on a transformative journey together to discover the profound truth about living whole, regardless of our relationship status.

This book isn't just another guide about surviving singleness or patiently waiting for "the one." It's a new way of seeing life— a fresh lens that helps you embrace your power, passion, and purpose right where you are. Together, we'll learn how to turn what society calls a "waiting period" into a meaningful season of growth, joy, and purpose. Maybe you've felt the sting of those familiar questions: *"When will you get married?"* or *"Still single?"* Maybe you've battled loneliness, tried to balance your dreams and societal pressure, or felt left behind. Whatever your story, you are not alone — and you are certainly not incomplete. With insights from the Bible and practical lessons from everyday life, we'll walk through what it truly means to live well as a single person. You'll learn how to find your identity in Christ, break free from cultural myths, build financial strength, and cultivate deep, healthy relationships. Each chapter will give you both spiritual guidance and practical steps to help you live a fulfilled and purposeful life. You are not broken because you're single. You are not behind. You are not "less than" your married or partnered friends. Singleness can be one of the most powerful, productive, and spiritually rich seasons of life—if you choose to live it with intention. Singlehood is not God's backup plan for your life; it's His current assignment. If He has allowed it, He has appointed it.

In this book, you'll learn how to embrace singlehood as a blessing and a time to thrive. You'll gain self-awareness, set meaningful goals, and build a life filled with confidence, joy, and purpose.This message comes from a place of deep understanding and compassion. Whether you're newly single, have chosen this path, or have been waiting for a while, these pages are for you. Inside, you'll find wisdom, encouragement, and practical tools for overcoming loneliness, finding community, and living out your God-given purpose. My prayer is that as you read, you'll begin to see singleness in a new light. fresh perspectives on living wholly and purposefully in your current season. You'll discover strength in your identity in Christ, build unshakable confidence, and create a life that shines with meaning — one that isn't defined by relationship status but by divine purpose.

So take a deep breath, open your heart, and prepare to embark on this transformative journey. It's time to redefine singleness not as a period of lack or waiting, but as a season rich with opportunity for growth, impact, and divine purpose. Welcome to your journey of living whole—where every page turns toward discovering the powerful, passionate, and purposeful life God has designed for you.

Let's begin.

Chapter 1

Embracing God's Divine Identity: Your Worth Beyond Relationship Status

"I am self-sufficient in Christ's sufficiency."

The mirror reflects more than just your physical appearance. It reveals a masterpiece crafted by the Divine Artist, complete and whole in every way. Your identity, like a precious jewel, has its own worth that doesn't depend on your relationship status. It simply waits to be discovered and embraced in its fullness. Just as a jeweler carefully shapes and sets each stone, God has lovingly crafted every part of who you are. Every detail of your being reflects His purpose and design. In this chapter, we'll embark on a transformative journey to discover the profound truth about who you are—not through the world's standards or relationship status, but through God's unchanging perspective of who you truly are.

The struggle to define our worth beyond relationship status is a common human experience, one that resonates deeply with many of us. Society often presents a narrative that suggests completeness comes through romantic partnership, but Scripture paints a vastly different picture. In Colossians 2:10, we are reminded that we are "complete in Him" not needing any external factor to validate our existence or worth.

The journey of self-discovery and identity formation is particularly poignant in our single seasons. These times offer unique opportunities for deep introspection and spiritual growth that might otherwise be harder to access. Remember Moses' years in Midian, David's time in the wilderness, or Paul's period in Arabia—all seasons of apparent solitude that God used to shape these individuals for their divine purpose.

Like the stars of the night sky, your unique traits, gifts, and purpose have been intentionally placed by the Master Designer. God's craftsmanship in your life goes far deeper than outward appearances—it's embedded in your spiritual DNA, shaping you perfectly for the purpose He's prepared for your life.

In today's world, we often hear messages that measure our worth by relationship status or worldly success. Over time, those voices can weaken our trust in God's design and make us doubt our value. But just as a jeweler carefully sets each precious stone in its perfect place, God has lovingly shaped every part of who you are with purpose and precision. Your identity is not a blank canvas waiting to be filled by someone else's presence. Rather, it is already a masterpiece, signed by the Master Artist Himself. **Psalm 139:14** declares that we are "fearfully and wonderfully made," a truth that stands independent of our relationship status or life circumstances.

Payton's story resonates with many who have felt the weight of societal expectations and familial pressures regarding relationship status. Sitting in her car outside that wedding venue, fighting back tears after well-meaning relatives had bombarded her with questions about her single status, she felt the weight of societal expectations diminishing her accomplishments. Despite being a successful pediatric nurse who loved her career and served actively in her church, these achievements somehow felt hollow in the face of her singleness.

But that evening marked the beginning of her transformation. As she journaled her frustrations and opened her Bible, the truth about being fearfully and wonderfully made began to sink deeper than ever before. She started listing every truth she could find about her identity in Christ—**chosen**, **beloved**, **purposefully created**. The revelation that her worth wasn't waiting to be validated by a relationship, that Jesus had already established it changed everything.

This awareness led Payton to start a Bible study group for single professionals, where they explored their identity in Christ together. Her journey from struggling with her single status to mentoring younger singles at her church demonstrates how embracing our God-given identity releases us to fulfill our divine purpose.

You see, your identity isn't a temporary placeholder until a relationship comes along—it's the firm foundation upon which God builds His purpose for your life. You are His masterpiece, created anew in Christ Jesus to do the good works He planned long ago. This truth stands independent of your relationship status or life circumstances.

As we continue through this chapter, we'll explore practical steps for embracing your divine identity, understanding your unique purpose, and walking confidently in who God created you to be. Together, we'll discover how understanding our worth in Christ transforms not just how we view ourselves, but how we approach every aspect of our lives.

"For we are God's masterpiece. He has created us anew in Christ Jesus, so we can do the good things he planned for us long ago." - Ephesians 2:10

Remember, when God looks at you, He sees His masterpiece—complete, whole, and purposefully designed for this exact season of your life. Your journey of discovering and embracing this truth starts now.

Understanding Your Divine DNA: Created for Purpose

Just as every snowflake carries an intricate pattern that makes it unique, you carry within you a divine imprint that makes you distinctly and wonderfully you. This spiritual DNA goes beyond your look or personality—it reflects the very essence of who God created you to be and the purpose He has woven into your life.

Imagine an artist crafting a masterpiece, carefully selecting each color, each brush stroke, with deliberate intention. That's how your Creator has shaped you—with loving attention to every detail of your being. You are, as Scripture tells us, His masterpiece, created anew in Christ Jesus to do the good works He prepared in advance for you to do. This truth runs deeper than any circumstance, any relationship status, or any season of life you're in.

Your divine DNA is a profound spiritual reality that shapes every aspect of who you are and what you're called to do. Just as physical DNA carries unique genetic codes that determine traits and characteristics, your divine DNA contains God's intentional design for your purpose, gifts, and calling.[1] This truth stands independent of relationship status, rooted instead in your creation as an image-bearer of God (Genesis 1:26-27).

The concept of divine DNA reminds us that we are "fearfully and wonderfully made" (Psalm 139:14), crafted with intention and purpose by a loving Creator. This fundamental truth challenges the common misconception that our purpose somehow lies dormant until marriage or partnership. Instead, Scripture consistently affirms that every person is created on purpose and for a purpose (Ephesians 2:10).

In a world that often measures worth by relationship status or achievements, it's easy to lose sight of this profound truth. Society's messages can whisper that we're somehow incomplete or waiting for life to truly begin. But your divine DNA tells a different story—it speaks of your Creator, who delighted in making you exactly as you are and who placed within you everything needed for the unique calling He has on your life.

Think about the careful precision with which God has crafted you—your talents, your personality, your dreams, and even your struggles have all been allowed to shape you for His divine purpose. You're not a rough draft waiting to be edited or an unfinished work anticipating completion through a relationship. You are His completed masterpiece, carrying within you the capacity for a deep relationship with Him, meaningful service to others, and kingdom impact that only you can bring to the world in your distinct way.

Embracing this truth means recognizing that you're not waiting for life to begin—you're living it right now. Your divine DNA isn't what you do—it's t who you are as God's beloved child, created with intention, purpose, and matchless worth. In discovering and expressing this truth, you step more fully into the person God designed you to be, reflecting His glory in ways that only you can.

Understanding your Divine Design, your DNA encompasses three core elements:

- Your identity as God's beloved child
- Your unique spiritual gifts and natural talents
- Your specific calling and purpose in God's kingdom

This design isn't waiting to be activated by a relationship—it's already fully present within you, ready to be discovered and expressed. As Jesus demonstrated through His own life, singleness can be a powerful platform for living out divine purpose with focus and intentionality.

When you understand this divine DNA within you, it transforms how you view your single season. Rather than seeing it as a waiting period, you can embrace it as a sacred space where God is actively working through you, using your unique design to impact His kingdom in ways that may only be possible in this very season. You are His creation, His handiwork, crafted with purpose and released with power to live out the good works He has already prepared for you to do.

Breaking Free from Society's Definition of Worth

God has woven a unique spiritual signature into your being that cannot be replicated. This divine imprint carries His dreams, purposes, and calling for your life—crafted with intentional care and perfect wisdom before time began.

In today's world, we often hear subtle messages that link our worth to relationship status or life achievements. Over time, these ideas can quietly weaken our confidence in God's intentional design for us. Society often treats singleness as something temporary—a phase to move past or a problem to solve. This mindset can create unnecessary pressure and cause us to overlook the beauty and purpose that exist in every season of life. However, Scripture presents a radically different view. God has lovingly crafted every part of who you are with care, purpose, and intention. You see, you are God's masterpiece—His poiema, His work of art—created anew in Christ Jesus to do the good works He planned long ago. This truth isn't dependent on your relationship status or life circumstances. It's woven into the very fabric of who you are. Before you took your first breath, He thoughtfully selected every spiritual gift, every personality trait, and every passion that makes you uniquely you.[2]

The journey begins with understanding that your value isn't determined by whether you're single or married but by your identity as a beloved child of God. As Psalm 139:14 reminds us, you are "fearfully and wonderfully made"—a truth that stands independent of relationship status.

Embracing this truth requires a gentle but profound shift in perspective—from seeing yourself through society's shifting lens to recognizing your true identity as God's beloved masterpiece. Gen 1 v 27. Your journey of discovering this divine imprint might unfold in quiet moments of prayer, bold steps of faith into new opportunities, or deep encounters with God's heart for you. Each experience reveals another facet of His purpose woven into who you are.

Like a seed contains everything needed to become a mighty oak, you carry within you everything required to flourish and fulfill God's beautiful design for your life. You're not waiting for your life to begin—you're living it right now, carrying within you everything needed to fulfill God's beautiful design for this season.

Your worth isn't waiting to be activated by some future circumstance or relationship. It's already fully present within you, woven into your being by the Master Creator Himself. This divine imprint you carry holds something precious—the capacity for deep connection with God, meaningful service to others, creative expression, and kingdom impact that only you can bring to the world.

Cultivating Unshakeable Identity in Christ

The Master Weaver has crafted every thread of your being with exquisite purpose and perfect love, creating what we might call your divine DNA, not just the physical traits that make you recognizable, but the spiritual imprint that makes you irreplaceably you.

Long before He laid the foundations of the earth, God thoughtfully designed every aspect of who you are.[3] This purpose isn't activated by marriage or partnership—it's already fully present within you, waiting to be discovered and expressed.

Your divine DNA is like carrying God's specific blueprint for your life—your unique combination of gifts, passions, and calling that no one else can fulfill quite like you. When you begin to see yourself through this lens, the hollow messages about worth being tied to relationship status naturally fade away in light of this greater truth: you are complete in Christ, purposefully designed for this exact season.

At the core of your existence is your divine DNA. It speaks to not just who you are, but whose you are. Like a seed containing all it needs to become a mighty oak, you carry within you everything required to flourish and fulfill your God-given purpose—the capacity for a deep relationship with Him, meaningful service to others, creative expression, and kingdom impact that's uniquely yours to steward.

Embracing this truth invites us to see singleness not as a waiting room but as a sacred space where God can develop and deploy our unique design. It's in this season that we have unprecedented opportunities to discover the depths of who He created us to be, unrestricted by the demands and compromises that often come with partnership.

Your journey of discovering and living out your divine identity might unfold in many ways, through quiet moments of prayer, bold steps of faith into new opportunities, or personal encounters with God's Word that reveal His love for you. Every experience, whether joyful or difficult, helps uncover another part of His purpose for your life.

Remember, you're not waiting for your life to begin—you're living it right now, carrying within you everything needed to fulfill God's beautiful design for this season. Your divine DNA isn't just about what you do—it's about who you are as God's beloved child, created with intention, purpose, and matchless worth.

As we conclude this foundational chapter on embracing God's divine identity, let's pause and reflect. We began with the mirror—seeing beyond our reflection to recognize the masterpiece God created. Through Payton's story and our discussion of divine identity, we've learned that our worth isn't tied to our relationship status or what others think. It's anchored in being God's children.

Becoming confident in your identity in Christ isn't something that happens overnight. It's a lifelong process of learning, renewing, and growing. As you let God reshape your thinking, you begin to see yourself the way He sees you—His masterpiece, made new in Christ to do the good works He planned for you. So remember: your single season isn't a waiting room—it's a workshop. God is using this time to shape your character, refine your purpose, and draw you closer to Him. Your identity is already complete in Christ. You don't need a relationship or anyone else's approval to confirm your worth.

Action Steps:

- Start an "Identity in Christ" Journal. Each day for one week, write down one truth from Scripture about who God says you are (e.g., "I am a beloved child of God," "I am a masterpiece").
- Rewrite Your Mirror Reflection. Write Psalm 139:14 on a sticky note and place it on your mirror. Read it aloud every morning as a declaration of truth.
- Share Your Story. Have a conversation with a trusted friend about Payton's story and discuss where you each feel the pressure to find your identity outside of Christ.

Key Chapter Takeaways:

- Your worth is divinely established, not socially determined.
- Identity in Christ provides a foundation for purposeful living.

- Breaking free from cultural definitions requires intentional action.
- Every season holds an opportunity for growth and impact.

Reflection Questions:

- In what areas of your life have you been defining your worth through relationship status rather than through Christ?
- How might your perspective shift if you viewed your single season as a workshop rather than a waiting room?
- What specific steps can you take this week to align your self-view more closely with God's truth?
- In what ways can you begin using your complete identity in Christ to impact others?

Scriptures for Meditation:

- Ephesians 2:10: "For we are God's masterpiece, created in Christ Jesus for good works, which God prepared in advance for us to do."
- Colossians 2:10: "...and in Christ you have been brought to fullness."
- Psalm 139:14: "I praise you because I am fearfully and wonderfully made; your works are wonderful; I know that full well."

Prayer focus:

"Lord, thank you for creating me with purpose and establishing my worth through Your love. Help me to see myself as You see me; to embrace the identity You've given me, and to live confidently in the truth of who I am in You. Show me how to use this season for Your glory and my growth. Amen."

Chapter 2

Breaking Free: Overcoming Cultural Myths About Singleness

"Above all else, guard your heart, for everything you do flows from it."

In today's world, where relationship status often seems to determine a person's value, it's important to recognize that these cultural myths about singleness go against God's truth. The Bible tells a different story. In 1 Corinthians 7:32–35, the Apostle Paul describes singleness not as a burden, but as a gift—an opportunity for undivided devotion to the Lord. This chapter will help you identify these common myths, understand their impact on your life, and you how to replace them with biblical truth and practical wisdom so you can live in freedom and confidence.

Morgan knew this pressure well. Sitting in her aunt's living room at yet another family gathering, she held her coffee cup like a shield against the familiar questions about her love life. She was thriving in her career as a financial analyst, active in church leadership, and had just returned from a mission trip to Guatemala. Yet, despite all her achievements, she still felt reduced to her relationship status like her success was a mere consolation prize for not being married. That evening, after returning home, Morgan found herself reflecting on a recent Bible study about Paul's teachings on singleness in 1 Corinthians 7. The apostle's words about the unique advantages of undivided devotion to the Lord began to resonate with her in a new way. She realized she had been allowing cultural expectations to overshadow God's perspective on her season of life.[4]

Over the next few months, Morgan embarked on a journey of renewing her mind with biblical truth. She began to see how her singleness had actually enabled her to serve in ways she couldn't have otherwise—from spontaneous ministry opportunities to mentoring young women in her community. As she came to embrace God's view of her status, she found herself responding to family pressures in a different way. Instead of defensive explanations, she began sharing confidently about how God was using her life in its current season.

The transformation wasn't instant, but it was profound. Morgan's story illustrates how breaking free from cultural myths about singleness isn't just about changing our circumstances—it's about changing our perspective through the lens of God's truth.

As we journey through this chapter together, we'll explore how these cultural myths have shaped our understanding of singleness and discover powerful biblical truths that can set us free from their influence. We'll learn practical strategies for handling social pressure and family expectations while maintaining our joy and purpose in Christ.

Your worth isn't determined by your relationship status but by your identity as a beloved child of God. As Isaiah 43:1 reminds us, "Fear not, for I have redeemed you; I have called you by name; you are mine." Let's begin this journey of breaking free from cultural myths and stepping into the fullness of who God has called us to be.

Identifying and Challenging Cultural Myths: Understanding Common Misconceptions About Singleness

What if I told you that many of the things people believe about being single aren't actually true? Over time, these ideas have been passed down from generation to generation, shaping how we see ourselves and what we expect from life.[5] They can even influence our happiness and hold us back from fully embracing our potential. In this chapter, we'll uncover some of these common myths and see how God's truth brings a fresh, freeing perspective to each one.

Myth #1: To Be Single Is to Be Lonely

As Morgan looked around the room, it was easy to believe this one. The world tells us that romantic partnership is the ultimate cure for loneliness. But this is a misleading half-truth. Loneliness isn't the absence of a partner; it's the absence of a deep, authentic connection. I've spoken with many married people who confess to feeling profoundly lonely within their own homes. You can be in a crowd, or even in a marriage, and feel utterly disconnected.

The Truth from God's Word: God designed us for community, not just for coupleship. Your single season is a unique and powerful time to build a diverse "family" of deep friendships and meaningful bonds. The quality of your relationships matters far more than your relationship status. Jesus Himself, a single man, was surrounded by a rich community of friends who shared life with Him. This season is your invitation to cultivate those "iron sharpens iron" friendships that will sustain you for a lifetime.

"God sets the lonely in families; he leads out the prisoners with singing" (Psalm 68:6).

Myth #2: You're Single Because Something Is Wrong with You

As another friend at the shower announced her engagement, Chloe felt a familiar sting. The myth whispered, *"See? Everyone else figures it out. You're still single because you're flawed, lacking, or just not good enough."* This is perhaps the cruellest myth of all because it turns a simple life circumstance into a personal indictment. It ignores the countless factors that shape our lives—our values, priorities, timing, and choices.[6]

The Truth from God's Word: Your relationship status has absolutely no bearing on your worth or lovability in God's eyes. You are not a problem to be fixed. The Bible is clear: you are complete in Christ (Colossians 2:10), not in a spouse. Not at a future wedding. Not when someone finally "chooses" you. Your wholeness is a present reality, secured by the God who fearfully and wonderfully made you.

Myth #3: All Singles Must Be Desperately Searching

The prevailing cultural narrative assumes that every single person is on a constant, desperate quest for a partner. But is that true? Many people choose singleness for a season for powerful and valid reasons—to focus on their calling, to heal from past wounds, or to simply enjoy a period of undivided focus and growth. This myth disrespects personal choice and implies that a self-sufficient life is not a fulfilling one.

The Truth from God's Word: Romantic love is a beautiful gift, but it doesn't have to be sought from a place of desperation. In fact, a life lived with purpose and wholeness is often the most attractive.[7] More importantly, God may be calling you to a season of focused devotion. Paul even encouraged this, highlighting the unique spiritual advantages of being undistracted by worldly concerns (1 Corinthians 7:32-35). Your season isn't about a frantic search; it can be about a holy focus.

Myth #4: A Partner Is Necessary for Wholeness

This is the "you complete me" myth. It places an impossible burden on another human to be the source of our fulfillment and wholeness. This mindset not only robs us of the journey of self-discovery but also sets us up for any future relationship failure.

The Truth from God's Word: You are already whole. A partner can *complement* you, but they cannot *complete* you. Jesus, the most complete and purpose-filled person to ever walk the earth, lived His entire life single. Your completeness comes from your identity in Him. When you live from that place of wholeness, you bring strength and health into every relationship you have, rather than looking for relationships to fix you.

"But he said to me, 'My grace is sufficient for you, for my power is made perfect in weakness.'" (2 Corinthians 12:9)

Myth #5: A Single Life Lacks Meaning

This myth suggests that the deepest meaning in life is found within a romantic partnership. If we believe this, we put our purpose on hold, waiting for someone else to give our life significance.[8]

The Truth from God's Word: Your purpose was sealed before you were even born (Jeremiah 1:5). Meaning doesn't come from another person; it comes from aligning your life with your Creator's design. You can find profound purpose and contentment right now—in your career, your creative passions, your service to others, and your spiritual journey. Your life doesn't become meaningful when someone loves you; it becomes meaningful when you live out the love God has already placed within you.

Myth #6: You Are "Behind" in Life

In our milestone-obsessed society, it's easy for singles to feel like they are falling behind as friends get married, buy houses, and have children.[9] This comparison game can lead to feelings of self-pity, bitterness, and a constant sense of being "less than."

The Truth from God's Word: Everyone's path is unique. There is no divine "timeline" you are failing to meet. The Bible says there is a time for everything (Ecclesiastes 3:1), and that includes the specific season you are in right now. Embrace it and find joy in it. This phase will pass, and you can't rewind the clock. God is not in a hurry, and He is never late. Your life is happening now. Your dreams and goals don't have to wait for a plus-one. Your call doesn't begin after the ring. This is not a pause; it is a power move.

As you reflect on these myths, ask yourself:

- Which cultural stories about singleness have most influenced how you see yourself?
- How has God used your single season to develop your character or serve others?
- What unique opportunities does your current season provide for kingdom impact?

- What beliefs have I carried about my own singleness that don't align with Scripture?

Meditate on these powerful truths from Scripture over the myths:

- Isaiah 54:5 - The Lord is your maker and husband.
- 1 Corinthians 7:17 - Living the life God has assigned
- Jeremiah 29:11—God's plans for hope and future

Challenging these cultural myths isn't just about changing our thinking—it's about embracing God's perspective and living purposefully in our current season. Your value comes from being God's beloved child, not your relationship status.

In the words of Paul, "I have learned to be content whatever the circumstances" (Philippians 4:11). This contentment flows not from perfect circumstances but from understanding our completeness in Christ and embracing the unique purpose He has for each season of our lives.

Redefining Singlehood: God's Perspective on Singleness and Purpose

What if I told you that God's view of singleness is radically different from our cultural assumptions? While society often paints singleness as a waiting room for life to begin, God's perspective reveals it as a sacred season filled with divine purpose and extraordinary potential.[10]

Time and again throughout Scripture, we see how God elevates the single life far beyond our limited human understanding. Take Jesus Christ, for example—the central figure of our faith lived His entire earthly ministry as a single man, demonstrating that life's most profound impact requires no marital status. His example shatters our modern assumptions about needing marriage for fulfillment or significance.

The Apostle Paul takes this even further, presenting singleness not as a burden to be endured but as a gift that unlocks unique opportunities for serving God. In 1 Corinthians 7, he writes with refreshing clarity about the advantages of singleness, pointing out how unmarried individuals can serve the Lord with undivided devotion. This biblical framework transforms our view of singleness from a state of waiting into a season of active purpose and divine calling.

Consider these life-changing truths about God's perspective on singleness:

- Completeness in Christ
- "For in Christ all the fullness of the Deity lives in bodily form, and in Christ you have been brought to fullness" (Colossians 2:9-10).
- Your wholeness comes from your relationship with Christ, not your relationship status.
- God sees you as complete and fully equipped for your current season.

Action Steps:

To break free from these cultural myths, consider these practical steps:

- Start a gratitude journal focusing on the unique opportunities your single season provides.
- Identify societal messages that have influenced your self-worth and replace these messages with biblical truth.

- Develop healthy boundaries with those who reinforce limiting beliefs.
- Engage in activities that align with your purpose and values.
- Create intentional friendships across different life stages
- Develop a personal mission statement focused on your current season
- Build a support system of like-minded singles and mentors
- Identify and pursue ministry opportunities that leverage your flexibility

Key Chapter Takeaway:

- Your life becomes meaningful when you live out God's love.
- You are whole by yourself. A partner can only complement you, but cannot complete you. A complete self brings fulfilment to your life and that of others.
- Meaning in life comes from within yourself, not from others, and it takes courage to cultivate it one moment at a time.
- This phase will pass, and you can't rewind the clock. Your life is happening now; make the most of it.

Reflection Questions:

- How have cultural myths influenced your view of your single season?
- What specific truths from God's Word can replace these myths in your thinking?
- In what ways has God uniquely positioned you to serve and impact others in this season?

- How can you better steward the freedom and flexibility of your single season?

Scriptures To Meditate On:

- 1 Corinthians 7:32-35 - The unique advantages of undivided devotion
- Isaiah 43:1 - You are called by name and belong to God
- Philippians 4:11-13 - Finding contentment in every season

Prayer Focus:

My Lord and my God, thank you dearly for the life you have given me. Thank you for those you have surrounded me with. I pray for wisdom to set healthy boundaries with those who reinforce limiting beliefs and help me replace those beliefs with your promises and the Word of God, in Jesus' name, Amen.

Chapter 3

Cultivating Wholeness: The Journey to Self-Discovery and Purpose

"Let each one live the life which the Lord has assigned him, and to which God has called him."

On this sacred journey of self-discovery, we learn that true wholeness isn't found in relationships or external circumstances but in knowing who we are in Christ and understanding the purpose for which we were created. Like a gardener who knows that every seed already holds its full potential, we must realize that God has planted within us everything we need to grow and flourish. Wholeness begins when we understand that we are not incomplete, waiting for someone else to make us whole. We are already complete in Christ—equipped with unique gifts, talents, and purpose meant to be nurtured and expressed in this season.

As Paul reminds us in Colossians 2:10, we are "complete in Him, who is the head of all principality and power." Just as Elijah discovered in his journey from questioning to purpose, God often uses our single season as a divine appointment for deeper self-discovery and ministry impact. Sitting in his study surrounded by self-help books and career planning guides, Elijah felt overwhelmed by the pressure to "figure it all out." His successful career in finance seemed hollow without the traditional markers of adult life that his married friends possessed. However, through prayer and reflection, Elijah experienced a profound shift in perspective that would transform his understanding of purpose and wholeness.

Instead of viewing his single season as a waiting period, he began to see it as a divine appointment for deep personal growth and ministry. As he started volunteering at his church's youth program, he discovered his gift for mentoring young professionals and began pursuing a certification in financial coaching. Through this process, Elijah realized that what he had perceived as a "delay" in marriage was actually God's perfect timing, allowing him to develop his gifts and impact others in ways he never imagined.

His journey from questioning his purpose to embracing his season of singleness became a powerful testimony of how God uses every season for our growth and His glory. Like Elijah, many of us may find ourselves at similar crossroads, wondering if we're somehow behind in life's timeline. Yet the truth remains—this season of singleness holds unique opportunities for discovering our authentic selves and aligning our lives with God's divine purpose.

Embracing our wholeness in Christ provides us with the secure foundation necessary to develop emotional intelligence and self-awareness—crucial tools for personal growth and fostering meaningful relationships.[11] This deep understanding of ourselves creates space for authentic connection with others while maintaining healthy boundaries. Through this journey, we learn to align our daily choices with God's purpose, transforming ordinary moments into opportunities for extraordinary impact.

In this chapter, we'll explore practical steps for cultivating wholeness while single, examining how emotional intelligence and self-awareness serve as vital tools for personal growth. Through biblical wisdom, reflective exercises, and real-life examples, we'll uncover how nurturing wholeness in Christ leads to a life of power, passion, and purpose—regardless of relationship status.

As we begin this exploration of wholeness and purpose, remember the words of Jeremiah 29:11: "For I know the plans I have for you," declares the Lord, "plans to prosper you and not to harm you, plans to give you hope and a future." This promise holds true in every season of life, including your single season. Let's embark on this journey of self-discovery together, confident that God is already at work, shaping you into the person He created you to be.

Understanding Biblical Wholeness: Complete in Christ

The mirror reflects more than just your image—it shows a masterpiece crafted by the Divine Artist, complete and whole in every way. Your identity, like a precious jewel, holds intrinsic value that exists independently of your relationship status, waiting to be discovered and embraced in its fullness.

Biblical wholeness is a profound state of being, complete and lacking nothing through our union with Christ. This completeness isn't dependent on relationship status, achievements, or life circumstances—it flows from our identity as children of God. As we embrace this truth, we begin to see ourselves through heaven's lens rather than society's expectations.

Too often, we view wholeness through what appears to be missing in our lives—an empty chair at the dinner table, a vacant space in our bed, or an unfulfilled dream in our heart. However, biblical wholeness speaks to a deeper truth—that in Christ, we already possess everything needed for life and godliness. This completeness encompasses every dimension of our being—spiritual, emotional, mental, physical, and relational.

Biblical wholeness means "nothing missing, nothing broken, complete in every part, through and through, no part wanting or unsound." This isn't about achieving perfection through self-improvement efforts, but rather embracing the transformative work Christ has already accomplished. As 2 Corinthians 5:17 declares, *"Therefore, if anyone is in Christ, the new creation has come: The old has gone, the new is here!"*

When we truly understand that we're already complete in Christ, it changes how we see and live our lives. We stop chasing wholeness through relationships or achievements and start living from the wholeness we already have. This shift frees us to pursue our purpose and passions without the pressure to prove our worth or find completion in anything outside of God. Embracing this truth doesn't mean denying our natural desire for companionship or pretending that loneliness doesn't exist. Rather, it means approaching these feelings with confidence in who we are, instead of seeking validation through others. When we know we are whole in Christ, we can form relationships from a place of fullness—not need. This understanding revolutionizes how we view our single season. Instead of seeing it as a time of lack or waiting, we begin to see it as an opportunity to experience and express the fullness we already have in Christ. Our completeness isn't waiting to be validated by a relationship—it's already established through our identity in Him.[12]

Spiritual wholeness forms the foundation, bringing reconciliation with God and peace that transcends understanding (Philippians 4:7). This spiritual completeness then flows into emotional wholeness, freeing us from guilt, shame, and fear while embracing joy and hope. Mental wholeness follows as we renew our minds according to God's truth (Romans 12:2). Physical and relational wholeness also find their proper context in Christ.[13] While we may experience physical limitations or relational disappointments, our fundamental completeness in Christ remains unshaken. This truth empowers us to foster healthy relationships from a place of fullness rather than need.

The journey to embracing biblical wholeness involves daily choices to align our thinking with God's truth. It means actively challenging cultural messages that suggest we're somehow incomplete without a romantic partner. It requires developing new patterns of thought that affirm our completeness in Christ while remaining open to the beautiful possibility of sharing life with another person.

As we deepen our understanding of biblical wholeness, we discover that being complete in Christ provides a secure foundation necessary for developing emotional intelligence and cultivating healthy relationships. From this place of wholeness, we can pursue our purpose with confidence, knowing that our value and completeness are already settled in heaven's court.

You are not waiting to become whole—you are discovering the wholeness that has been yours all along in Christ. This truth liberates you to live fully in your present season while remaining open to all that God has for your future.

Emotional Intelligence and Self-Awareness: Tools for Personal Growth

The journey toward wholeness requires more than just understanding our identity in Christ—it demands developing the emotional wisdom to navigate life's complexities with grace and purpose.[14] Emotional intelligence and self-awareness serve as vital tools God has given us to understand ourselves more deeply and steward our relationships with wisdom.

Like a skilled navigator who must understand the terrain before charting a course, we must develop awareness of our emotions to grow in maturity and purpose. This involves recognizing our emotional patterns, understanding our typical responses, and identifying areas where God is calling us to grow. The Scriptures provide numerous examples of individuals who demonstrated this kind of emotional wisdom—from David's raw honesty in the Psalms to Paul's remarkable insight into his own strengths and weaknesses.

Emotional intelligence encompasses four key domains that shape our overall well-being: self-awareness (knowing our own heart), self-management (stewarding our emotions), social awareness (understanding others), and relationship management (navigating connections with wisdom).[15] These components align beautifully with biblical principles of self-examination and growing in relationship wisdom.

Developing self-awareness begins with creating space for honest reflection. This might look like starting a daily journal to track emotional patterns, practicing mindfulness during daily activities, or seeking regular feedback from trusted mentors and friends. Remember that this journey isn't about suppressing emotions but understanding them as God-given indicators that help us navigate life's challenges with wisdom.

Scripture provides a rich foundation for emotional intelligence through principles such as:

- Self-examination (Lamentations 3:40)
- Emotional honesty before God (Psalm 139:23-24)
- Wisdom in relationships (Proverbs 22:24-25)
- Self-control (Galatians 5:22-23)

As we grow in emotional intelligence, we learn to recognize and manage our emotions before they take control. This awareness helps us build deeper, more genuine relationships and make choices that align with our values and purpose.[16] It also allows us to handle conflict with grace while maintaining healthy boundaries—skills that are vital for thriving in any season of life.

To develop emotional intelligence, start with small, practical steps: set aside time each day for reflection through prayer and journaling, create an "emotional awareness map" to identify your common triggers and reactions, and seek guidance from mentors or counselors who can support your growth. The goal isn't to be perfect—it's to keep growing, becoming more aware of how your emotions influence your decisions and relationships. The beauty of this journey is that God doesn't expect us to figure it out alone. The Holy Spirit serves as our internal teacher, helping us discern our emotions and respond with wisdom. As Psalm 139:23-24 reminds us, we can invite God into this process of self-discovery:

"Search me, O God, and know my heart; test me and know my anxious thoughts."

Embracing emotional intelligence as a spiritual practice transforms how we approach relationships, decisions, and daily challenges. Rather than being tossed about by emotional waves, we learn to navigate them with increasing skill and wisdom. This growth equips us to live out our purpose with greater clarity and impact, regardless of our relationship status.

Developing emotional intelligence is a journey, not a destination. Each step forward in self-awareness brings us closer to living authentically and purposefully in our current season. As we continue growing in these areas, we become better positioned to embrace all that God has for us—today and in the future.

Aligning Your Daily Life with Divine Purpose: Creating a Vision for Your Life

The journey of aligning your daily life with divine purpose begins with a profound understanding that every moment holds sacred potential. Just as an artist sees the masterpiece within an unmarked canvas, God considers the fullness of who you're becoming even as you navigate this present season. As Jeremiah 29:11 reminds us, "For I know the plans I have for you," declares the Lord, "plans to prosper you and not to harm you, plans to give you hope and a future."

Rather than viewing this season as a waiting period, embrace it as a divine appointment for clarifying your purpose and aligning your daily choices with God's calling. This time of singleness offers a unique opportunity for intentional living and deep self-discovery, allowing you to craft a vision that reflects both who you are and who God is calling you to become.

A vision statement serves as a compass, guiding your daily decisions and actions toward God's purpose for your life. Creating a vision for your life isn't merely a corporate exercise—it's a spiritual practice of seeking God's heart and documenting it with clarity and conviction. This process begins with quiet reflection and prayer, asking God to reveal His purposes for your life. Consider your core values, spiritual gifts, and the unique experiences that have shaped you. How might these elements combine to serve others and advance God's kingdom?

Vision without action remains merely a dream. The key to living purposefully lies in aligning your daily habits and choices with your larger vision. As Proverbs 29:18 states, "Where there is no vision, the people perish."

Begin each day with intentional prayer and Scripture reading. Keep a journal to document your spiritual journey and record your insights. Review your activities weekly to ensure they align with your vision, and reflect monthly on your progress and any necessary adjustments.

Certain mindsets can prevent us from fully embracing and pursuing our divine vision—such as comparing our journey to others', fearing to step out in faith, waiting for perfect circumstances, or allowing others' expectations to overshadow God's calling. Remember, you're already a whole person, capable of pursuing God's purposes right where you are. Living in alignment with God's purpose flows naturally from the wholeness we have in Christ and grows stronger as we develop emotional intelligence. When we understand who we are in Him and learn to manage our emotions with wisdom, we become better equipped to live out the unique vision He's placed within us. Each day becomes an opportunity to step more fully into the purpose for which we were created. As we conclude this journey of cultivating wholeness, remember—self-discovery and purpose aren't detours from life's path; they *are* the path. In this chapter, we've uncovered powerful truths about biblical wholeness, emotional intelligence, and divine purpose—truths that can transform how we experience our single season. Embracing our completeness in Christ gives us the firm foundation needed to grow in self-awareness and emotional maturity.[17] As we grow in understanding who we are in Him, we learn to navigate our emotions with wisdom and grace. From that place of stability, we begin to align our daily lives more closely with God's divine plan.[18]

The stories we've shared, from Elijah's transformation from questioning to purpose-driven living, to the practical tools for developing emotional intelligence, all point to a fundamental truth: wholeness is not found in external circumstances, but in our deep connection with Christ and our understanding of our divine purpose.

Action Steps:

- Create a "Wholeness Journal" to document your journey of growth and discovery.
- Develop a morning routine that reinforces your completeness in Christ.
- Write a personal vision statement aligned with God's purpose for your life.

- Identify one area of emotional intelligence to focus on this month
- Share your journey with a trusted friend or mentor for accountability.
- Regular monthly check-ins help evaluate progress and celebrate small wins while maintaining focus on the larger vision.
- Most importantly, remain open to the Holy Spirit's guidance as He transforms your vision into reality.

Key Chapter Takeaways:

- Biblical wholeness is our inheritance in Christ, not a destination we must strive to reach.
- Emotional intelligence and self-awareness are God-given tools for personal growth.
- Our daily choices can actively align with divine purpose when we operate from a place of wholeness.

Reflection Questions:

- How has your understanding of wholeness evolved through reading this chapter?
- How does my current routine reflect or contradict God's calling?
- What specific areas of emotional intelligence do you feel led to develop further?
- In what ways can you begin aligning your daily routines with God's purpose for your life?
- How am I using my single season to actively pursue God's vision?
- What limiting beliefs about wholeness do you need to surrender to God?

Scriptures To Meditate On:

Ground yourself in Scripture as you walk this path:

- Philippians 3:14—"I press on toward the goal to win the prize for which God has called me heavenward in Christ Jesus."
- Psalm 37:23—"The Lord makes firm the steps of the one who delights in him."
- Proverbs 16:9—"In their hearts humans plan their course, but the Lord establishes their steps."
- Romans 12:2—"Do not conform to the pattern of this world, but be transformed by the renewing of your mind."

This journey of cultivating wholeness is not about becoming someone different—it's about embracing who God has already created you to be. As you move forward from this chapter, carry with you the truth that you are complete in Christ, equipped with everything needed for this season of life.

Your single season is not a waiting room for life to begin—it's a sacred space for discovering and expressing the unique purpose God has placed within you. Continue to embrace this journey with courage, knowing that every step toward greater wholeness is a step toward living out your divine calling.

Prayer focus:

Father, thank you for the gift of wholeness in Christ. Lord, help me to embrace this truth deeply and live from a place of completeness rather than one of lack. Guide me as I develop emotional intelligence and align my daily life with Your divine purpose. May I walk in the confidence of knowing that I am exactly where You want us to be, fully equipped for every good work You have prepared for me, in Jesus' name, Amen.

Chapter 4

Sacred Solitude: Finding Joy in the Present Season

"Those who wait for the Lord will gain new strength and renew their power."

The gentle whisper of silence holds more wisdom than the loudest crowd, yet many of us run from its embrace, filling our lives with endless noise and distraction. In our fast-paced world where connection often means constant digital engagement, learning to embrace sacred solitude isn't just a spiritual discipline—it's a vital practice for maintaining our emotional and spiritual well-being. Like a seed that must be planted alone in the dark earth before it can flourish into a mighty tree, our seasons of solitude hold within them the potential for extraordinary growth and transformation.

In today's hyperconnected world, we often mistake being alone for being lonely, failing to recognize the sacred invitation that solitude offers. This divine appointment with ourselves and our Creator offers an irreplaceable opportunity for profound soul work, unencumbered worship, and transformative self-discovery. The Psalmist understood this profound truth when he wrote, "Be still, and know that I am God" (Psalm 46:10), reminding us that sometimes we must quiet the external noise to hear the internal whispers of divine wisdom.

Solitude, when embraced with intention, becomes a sanctuary where we can explore the depths of our relationship with God without distraction. It's in these quiet moments that we often discover our truest selves and catch a glimpse of God's grandest purposes for our lives. As Jesus himself demonstrated through His regular retreats to solitary places (Luke 5:16), there is supernatural strength to be found in chosen solitude.

I remember a particularly challenging period in my life when I found myself alone in a new city, far from family and familiar faces. The silence of my apartment felt deafening, and the weekends stretched endlessly before me. One morning, feeling particularly isolated, I decided to take a different approach to my solitude. Instead of filling the quiet with noise from television or social media, I created what I now call my 'Sacred Moment' ritual. I began with prayer and meditation, followed by journaling my thoughts and dreams.

As weeks passed, these solitary moments became precious opportunities for self-discovery and spiritual growth. Through this intentional practice, I discovered hidden talents, processed deep emotions, and developed a stronger sense of purpose. What started as a dreaded experience of loneliness transformed into a cherished time of personal development and divine connection. "In the silence, I've found clarity about my purpose, healing from past hurts, and a deeper connection with God that I never experienced in all my years of busy activities." This journey taught me that solitude, when embraced with intention, becomes not just bearable but beautiful—a sacred space where God's presence becomes more tangible and His purpose clearer.

The beauty of sacred solitude lies not in the absence of others, but in the presence of purpose. It's a divine invitation to deepen our spiritual roots, strengthen our emotional resilience, and cultivate a rich inner life that sustains us through every season.[19] As we learn to embrace these moments of sacred solitude, we discover that being alone doesn't mean being lonely—it means being available for some of God's most profound work in our lives.

In the chapters that follow, we'll explore practical ways to transform your solitary moments into opportunities for growth, joy, and divine connection. You'll learn how to create meaningful rituals that honor your alone time, develop spiritual disciplines that deepen your faith, and discover the unique gifts that this season of life holds for you.

The Divine Purpose of Solitude: Understanding God's Purpose in Alone Seasons

In the gentle rhythms of life, God orchestrates seasons of solitude not as empty spaces to endure, but as divine appointments crafted for extraordinary transformation and deeper communion.[20] These sacred moments of aloneness, when embraced with intention, become powerful catalysts for spiritual growth and self-discovery. Just as Jesus regularly withdrew to solitary places for prayer and communion with the Father (Luke 5:16), we too are invited to recognize that time alone with God isn't merely beneficial—it's essential for spiritual vitality.

Solitude differs fundamentally from loneliness in its nature and purpose. While loneliness often stems from a painful sense of disconnection, solitude is an intentional state where we encounter God's presence in profound ways.[21] As Richard Foster wisely notes, "While loneliness is inner emptiness, solitude is inner fulfillment." This vital distinction helps us approach our alone seasons not as periods of lack, but as opportunities for divine encounter.

Consider how Jesus prepared for pivotal ministry moments by withdrawing to solitary places (Luke 6:12). Before selecting His disciples, facing crucifixion, or following significant miracles, He prioritized these sacred moments of solitude. His example teaches us that solitude isn't a passive waiting period but an active space for spiritual preparation and divine direction.

In these quiet moments, God accomplishes several vital purposes in our lives:

- Deepening our communion with Him through uninterrupted worship and prayer
- Strengthening our spiritual foundation through meditation on His Word
- Clarifying our purpose and calling through divine whispers
- Healing emotional wounds in His gentle presence
- Developing spiritual discernment through practised listening

To embrace these sacred appointments with intention, consider creating dedicated spaces and times for solitude in your daily life. This might mean establishing a morning routine of prayer before the day begins, finding a quiet spot in nature for regular reflection, or setting aside evening hours for journaling and processing the day's events with God. The key is consistency and intentionality in these practices.

Like David, who processed his deepest emotions before God in solitude (Psalm 25:16), we too can transform our alone moments into powerful encounters with divine love. These seasons become sacred spaces where God shapes our character, heals our hearts, and prepares us for His purposes.

As you cultivate these practices of sacred solitude, remember that being alone with God is actually the richest form of companionship available to us. It's in these quiet moments that we often hear His voice most clearly, feel His presence most deeply, and understand His purpose most profoundly.

Your season of solitude isn't a waiting room—it's a workshop where God is crafting something beautiful in you. As you learn to embrace these moments, you'll discover that what once felt like isolation can become the very ground where your spiritual life flourishes most abundantly.

From Loneliness to Wholeness: Transforming Quiet Moments into Joy

The transformative journey from loneliness to wholeness begins with a profound shift in perspective—recognizing that our quiet moments hold divine purpose rather than emptiness. Like a master artist who sees potential in a blank canvas, God invites us to view our solitude not as a void to be filled, but as a sacred space where extraordinary growth and joy can flourish.

Loneliness often stems from viewing solitude through the lens of lack rather than opportunity. Scripture reveals that Jesus frequently sought solitude for spiritual renewal and divine communion (Luke 5:16). These moments weren't characterized by emptiness, but by a purposeful connection with the Father.[22]

Similarly, our quiet moments can become sacred spaces for transformation when we shift our perspective from isolation to invitation.

This transformation requires intentional engagement with three key elements: perspective, practice, and purpose. First, we must challenge the cultural narrative that equates being alone with being incomplete, demonstrating that these moments can become catalysts for spiritual vitality rather than sources of despair.

The practical journey involves creating sacred rhythms that honor both our need for solitude and our desire for meaningful connection. This might include:

- Establishing a morning ritual of prayer and meditation before the day begins
- Journaling to process emotions and capture divine insights
- Taking contemplative walks in nature
- Creating a dedicated space for quiet reflection and worship
- Developing new skills or exploring interests that bring joy

These practices aren't merely activities to fill time—they're investments in our spiritual and emotional well-being that allow us to experience the "fullness of joy" promised in God's presence (Psalm 16:11).

Purpose emerges as we begin to see our solitude as a divine appointment rather than a waiting room. Just as a seed requires darkness and isolation to transform into something beautiful, our quiet seasons often contain the very conditions needed for profound personal growth. This understanding allows us to approach our alone time not with dread, but with anticipation of what God might reveal or develop within us.[23]

The journey to wholeness also involves learning to distinguish between solitude and isolation. While isolation leads to stagnation, intentional solitude creates space for:

- Deeper communion with God through uninterrupted worship
- Processing emotions and experiences with divine wisdom
- Discovering and developing personal gifts
- Building emotional resilience and self-awareness
- Finding clarity about life direction and purpose

As we embrace these purposes, our quiet moments begin to overflow with meaning rather than emptiness. We discover that joy isn't dependent on external circumstances or companions but springs from our growing relationship with God and understanding of our intrinsic worth in Him.

Practical steps for cultivating joy in solitude include:

- Starting each day with gratitude and worship
- Creating beauty in your personal space
- Engaging in activities that nurture your spirit
- Maintaining a "joy journal" to document growth and blessings
- Developing meaningful spiritual disciplines

Transformation rarely happens overnight. Like any journey worth taking, moving from loneliness to wholeness requires patience, persistence, and grace for ourselves along the way. As we learn to embrace our solitude as sacred space, we often find that what once felt like a burden becomes a blessing—a cherished time where we experience God's presence most profoundly and discover the unique joy He has prepared for us in this season.

Your quiet moments aren't empty spaces to endure, they're holy ground where God is actively working to shape you into who He created you to be. As you learn to embrace these moments with intention and expectancy, you'll discover that true wholeness isn't found in the absence of loneliness but in the presence of purpose, and genuine joy emerges not from perfect circumstances but from perfect trust in the One who walks with you through every season.

Creating Sacred Spaces: Practical Steps for Meaningful Solitude

Creating sacred spaces begins with understanding that our environment profoundly impacts our spiritual and emotional well-being.[24] As we read in 1 Kings 19:11-13, even Elijah encountered God not in the wind, earthquake, or fire, but in the gentle whisper—reminding us that sacred spaces often facilitate our ability to hear God's still, small voice.[25]

The process of establishing meaningful spaces for solitude starts with intentional selection. This doesn't require an entire room—even a small corner of your bedroom or a comfortable chair by a window can become a sanctuary for spiritual reflection.

Consider these essential elements when creating your sacred space:

- Natural light or gentle artificial lighting
- A comfortable place to sit or kneel
- Your Bible, journal, and spiritual materials

- Elements that inspire peace (plants, artwork, or meaningful symbols)
- Protection from interruptions and distractions

Once you've chosen your location, prepare it with intention. Begin by physically cleaning the area, removing clutter and unnecessary items.[26] This physical clearing often parallels the internal clearing we seek in our quiet moments with God. As we read in 2 Corinthians 7:1, we are called to *"purify ourselves from everything that contaminates body and spirit."*

Establishing sacred rituals helps transform ordinary moments into divine encounters. These practices shouldn't feel burdensome; instead, they should naturally flow from your desire to connect with God. As Psalm 46:10 reminds us to "Be still and know that I am God," our sacred spaces become places where we intentionally practice this stillness.

Consider incorporating these elements into your sacred time[27]:

- Begin with silence and deep breathing.
- Read scriptures or devotional material
- Practice gratitude and reflection
- Write your thoughts and prayers

Consistency in using your sacred space strengthens its significance in your spiritual journey.[28] Like the priests who maintained the temple's sanctity (2 Chronicles 29:15-16), we too should regularly tend to our sacred spaces. This includes both physical maintenance and spiritual refreshment.

Your sacred space is not about creating a perfect environment but about fostering a place where you can consistently meet with God and nurture your spiritual life. The goal isn't to impress others but to create an environment where you feel at home with your spirit and can hear God's voice clearly.

Reflect on these questions as you establish your sacred space:

- Where in my home could I create a dedicated space for solitude with God?
- What would help me focus on God's presence?
- How can I protect and prioritize my time in this sacred space?

As you develop this practice, you'll find that these moments of sacred solitude become anchors in your day, grounding you in God's presence and purpose for your life. Your sacred space becomes not just a physical location but a spiritual haven where transformation occurs and divine encounters become regular occurrences.

Through consistent use of your sacred space, what begins as a simple corner or quiet spot can evolve into holy ground—a place where, like Moses before the burning bush, you regularly encounter the living God. Let your sacred space become a testimony to the truth that in stillness and solitude, we often find our greatest strength and clearest direction.

As we conclude this chapter on sacred solitude, we're reminded that our quiet moments aren't mere gaps to be filled but divine appointments for profound transformation. Through intentional solitude, we discover that being alone doesn't equal being lonely—rather, it creates space for some of God's most extraordinary work in our lives.

Action Steps:

- Designate a specific area in your home for quiet reflection and prayer.
- Establish regular rhythms of solitude in your daily schedule.
- Keep a journal to document your journey and insights.
- Practice being fully present in your alone moments without digital distractions.
- Create meaningful rituals that honor your time with God.

Key Chapter Takeaway

- Solitude is a divine invitation, not an empty waiting room.
- Quiet moments become catalysts for spiritual growth when approached with intention.
- Creating sacred spaces facilitates deeper communion with God.
- Our alone seasons hold purpose beyond preparation for relationships.

Reflection Questions:

- How has your perspective on solitude shifted through reading this chapter?
- What specific practices resonate most with your current season?
- In what ways might God be using your quiet moments for divine purposes?
- What steps will you take to create more meaningful sacred spaces in your daily life?

Scriptures To Meditate On:

- "Be still and know that I am God" (Psalm 46:10).
- "But when you pray, go into your room, close the door, and pray" (Matthew 6:6).
- "Those who wait on the Lord shall renew their strength" (Isaiah 40:31).

As you move forward from this chapter, remember that your season of solitude isn't a punishment or something to fix—it's a sacred opportunity to draw closer to God and experience deep personal growth. The practices and principles we've explored aren't just ways to pass the time; they're meaningful investments in your spiritual well-being—seeds that will bear fruit in every season of your life.

Prayer focus:

Heavenly Father, thank you for the gift of sacred solitude. Help me embrace these quiet moments not as periods of loneliness, but as opportunities for deeper communion with You. Transform my perspective on being alone, and teach me to find joy and purpose in these sacred spaces. Guide me as I implement these practices, and help me discover the unique purposes You have for this season of my life. In Jesus' name, amen.

Chapter 5

Building Your Life: Career, Calling, and Purpose

"Whatever you do, work at it with all your heart, as working for the Lord, not for human masters."

The journey of discovering your purpose extends far beyond the confines of your job title or relationship status—it's about uncovering the unique imprint God has placed on your life. In this sacred space of singleness, you have an extraordinary opportunity to explore, develop, and align your career path with your divine calling. Just as a master craftsman carefully shapes raw materials into something beautiful and purposeful, your career journey in this season of singleness presents a unique opportunity to craft a life of meaningful impact. The intersection of career and calling isn't merely about climbing corporate ladders or achieving professional milestones—it's about discovering how your work can become worship, your profession can align with purpose, and your influence can extend beyond the workplace.

In this chapter, we'll explore how to navigate the delicate balance between professional ambition and divine purpose, understanding that God's plan for your life encompasses both your career advancement and your spiritual growth. We'll examine practical strategies for discerning your calling, developing your gifts, and creating impact in your sphere of influence while maintaining spiritual alignment.

Let's look at Aurora's story:

Aurora sat in her office, staring at the promotion letter on her desk. The opportunity would mean relocating to another state and taking on significantly more responsibility. She had worked tirelessly to reach this point, but something felt unsettled in her spirit. The position would advance her career substantially, but would it align with the ministry work she had recently felt called to pursue?

For weeks, Aurora wrestled with the decision, spending countless hours in prayer and seeking counsel. Through this process, she began to understand that her career wasn't separate from her calling—it was part of it. She realized God had given her these skills and opportunities for a greater purpose. Instead of seeing it as an either/or decision, she began exploring how her corporate influence could become a platform for ministry.

Eventually, Aurora accepted the promotion but with a new perspective. She used her increased influence to start a workplace mentorship program, incorporating principles of servant leadership and ethical business practices. Her single season allowed her flexibility to pour extra hours into both her career and ministry without neglecting family obligations. Through this experience, Aurora discovered that God hadn't given her a choice between career and calling—He had given her a way to merge them both into her unique purpose.

This story illustrates how singles can leverage their freedom and flexibility to pursue both professional excellence and spiritual purpose, creating a life that honors God while making a significant impact in their chosen field.

Like Aurora, many singles find themselves at crossroads where professional opportunities and spiritual calling seem to diverge. However, the truth is that God often uses our careers as vessels for His purpose, creating platforms for influence and impact that extend far beyond our job descriptions. Your single season provides unique advantages in pursuing career excellence while developing your calling—advantages we'll explore throughout this chapter.

You will learn how to discern God's voice in career decisions, develop strategies for professional growth that honor biblical principles, and create a meaningful impact in whatever sphere of influence He has placed you. Whether you're just starting your career journey or seeking to pivot into a new territory, the principles we'll explore will help you align your professional path with God's purpose for your life.

Discerning Your Divine Purpose: Understanding the Difference Between Career and Calling

Have you ever noticed how a masterfully crafted symphony brings together different instruments, each playing its unique part to create something extraordinarily beautiful? Similarly, understanding the distinction between your career and calling is like discovering the unique melody God has written specifically for your life.

One of the most profound questions we face in our single season is understanding the difference between what we do for a living and what we're called to do with our lives. This distinction between career and calling isn't merely semantic—it's fundamental to living a life of purpose and impact.

As Frederick Buechner wisely observed, *"The place God calls you to is the place where your deep gladness and the world's deep hunger meet."* This profound insight helps us understand that while a career represents the practical path we take to earn our livelihood—our jobs, promotions, and professional achievements, a calling speaks to something far deeper. It's that gentle whisper from God, that divine purpose He's woven into the very fabric of who you are. As the Psalmist reminds us, *"For you created my inmost being, you knit me together in my mother's womb"* (Psalm 139:13).

Reflect on how God prepared Joseph throughout his career journey. From shepherd to slave to prison administrator to Egypt's second-in-command (career), each role developed skills he would need for his ultimate calling—saving nations during famine, Gen 41:39-41. His story teaches us that our careers aren't separate from God's plan but often serve as preparation for our greater purpose.

Daniel worked as a government official (career) while maintaining his prophetic calling (Daniel 2:48-49).

Lydia was a successful businesswoman (career) who used her position to advance the gospel (calling) (Acts 16:14-15).

In this season of singleness, you have a unique opportunity to explore and develop both your career and calling without divided commitments.[29] This isn't about choosing between success and service—it's about discovering how God can use your professional path as a platform for His purpose.

Here are three biblical principles to help you discern your divine purpose:

- **Listen for God's Leading**

    "Trust in the LORD with all your heart and lean not on your own understanding; in all your ways submit to him, and he will make your paths straight" (Proverbs 3:5-6). Take time in prayer and Scripture meditation to seek God's guidance about your purpose.

- **Steward Your Gifts and Talents**

    "Each of you should use whatever gift you have received to serve others, as faithful stewards of God's grace in its various forms" (1 Peter 4:10). What talents and abilities has God given you? How might these serve both your career and His kingdom?

- **Serve With Excellence**

    "Whatever you do, work at it with all your heart, as working for the Lord, not for human masters" (Colossians 3:23). Excellence in your career can become an act of worship when done with the right heart.

Your calling may not always look like traditional ministry. Perhaps God has placed you in the marketplace to be a light in the corporate world or given you technical skills to serve His people in unique ways.30 The key is recognizing that both your career and calling flow from the same source—His purpose for your life.

Take time to reflect on these questions:

- What activities bring you deep joy and seem to meet real needs around you?
- What gifts and talents do others consistently recognize in you?
- Where do you see the intersection of your professional skills and kingdom impact?
- How might God be using your current position to prepare you for your calling?

Be encouraged that God is intimately involved in both your professional development and spiritual journey. As Isaiah 30:21 promises, *"Whether you turn to the right or to the left, your ears will hear a voice behind you, saying, 'This is the way; walk in it.'"* Your single season provides a precious opportunity to explore this intersection of career and calling with focused attention.

Action Steps

- Create a purpose statement that articulates your understanding of your calling.
- List three ways you can begin expressing your calling within your current career.
- Identify one mentor who can guide you in aligning your career with your calling.
- Develop a weekly schedule that allows time for both professional growth and calling pursuit.

Discerning your divine purpose isn't about having everything figured out immediately. It's about walking in step with the Holy Spirit, being faithful with what He's given you today, and remaining open to how He might use both your career and calling to bring glory to His name. Trust that He who began a good work in you will carry it to completion (Philippians 1:6).

Strategic Career Building: Aligning Professional Goals with Kingdom Purpose

Just as a skilled potter carefully shapes clay with purpose and vision, your career journey in this season of singleness presents a precious opportunity to allow God to mould your professional path for His glory. Remember, dear friend, that your work isn't merely about climbing corporate ladders or achieving worldly success—it's about discovering how your daily labor can become an offering of worship to the Lord.

As Solomon wisely observed in Ecclesiastes 3:1, *"There is a time for everything, and a season for every activity under the heavens."* Your single season provides unique advantages for pursuing excellence in your career while staying aligned with God's purpose for your life. You have the gift of focused time and energy to explore how your professional skills can be used for Kingdom impact.

Consider these biblical principles as you build your career strategically:

- **Seek First His Kingdom**

    "But seek first his kingdom and his righteousness, and all these things will be given to you as well" (Matthew 6:33). Let this scripture guide your career decisions, remembering that when we prioritize God's purposes, He faithfully directs our professional paths.

- **Work as Unto the Lord**

    Your workplace is your mission field. Whether you're leading a team meeting or completing routine tasks, approach each responsibility as an opportunity to glorify God through excellence. As Colossians 3:23-24 reminds us, *"Whatever you do, work at it with all your heart, as working for the Lord, not for human masters."*

- **Steward Your Gifts Wisely**

    God has purposefully equipped you with specific talents and abilities. Your single season offers valuable space to develop these gifts through additional training, mentorship, or educational opportunities. Remember the parable of the talents—faithful stewardship leads to greater Kingdom impact.

Practical steps for aligning your career with Kingdom purpose:

- Start each workday with prayer, inviting God's guidance in your professional decisions.
- Seek mentorship from seasoned believers in your field who can offer both spiritual and professional wisdom.
- Look for opportunities to serve others through your work, whether through mentoring junior colleagues or using your skills to benefit your church or community.
- Regular heart checks to ensure your career ambitions remain surrendered to God's leading

As you build your career with Kingdom purpose, you'll likely face various challenges:

Ethical Dilemmas

- Stand firm in your convictions while maintaining professional relationships
- Seek wisdom through prayer and counsel when facing difficult decisions
- Remember that your integrity is more valuable than any career advancement

Work-Life Integration

- Establish boundaries that protect your spiritual well-being
- Create routines that support both professional excellence and personal growth
- Use your flexibility as a single person wisely

Career Transitions

- Trust God's timing in career changes
- Maintain faith during periods of uncertainty
- Stay focused on long-term Kingdom impact rather than short-term gains

Dear single believer, remember that God is deeply interested in your professional development. He wants to use your career not just as a means of provision but as a platform for Kingdom influence. As you navigate career decisions, trust that He who began a good work in you will be faithful to complete it (Philippians 1:6).

Take time to reflect on these questions prayerfully:

- How might God want to use my current role for His purposes?

- What skills or experiences am I gaining that could serve His Kingdom?
- Are my career goals aligned with His calling on my life?

Your professional journey isn't separate from your spiritual walk—it's an integral part of how God is shaping you for His purposes. In this season of singleness, embrace the opportunity to build your career with intentionality, always keeping your eyes fixed on Jesus, the author and perfecter of your faith.

Let us pray together:

"Heavenly Father, guide us in building careers that honor You. Help us see our work through Your eyes and use our professional influence for Your glory. Give us wisdom in making career decisions and courage to follow Your leading, even when it differs from worldly wisdom in Jesus' name, Amen."

Creating Impact Beyond the Workplace: Developing a Life of Meaningful Service

While the world measures success through promotions and profit margins, God's economy operates on a different scale—one where service and sacrifice create lasting impact that extends far beyond office walls. As singles, we're uniquely positioned to pour our lives into meaningful service that transforms both ourselves and our communities.

While professional success provides one avenue for impact, true significance often extends far beyond the walls of the workplace. As singles, we have a unique opportunity to leverage our time, energy, and resources for meaningful service that creates lasting change in our communities and world.[31] This calling to service isn't just about filling time or compensating for singleness—it's about embracing our divine purpose as agents of transformation.

Jesus in His earthly ministry consistently pointed to a life of service as the path to true greatness: *"Whoever wants to become great among you must be your servant"* (Matthew 20:26). This divine invitation to servanthood isn't a consolation prize for singleness—it's a holy calling that can reshape our understanding of purpose and impact.

Your single season provides distinct advantages for kingdom service that married individuals might find more challenging to navigate. The flexibility of your schedule, the autonomy in your decisions, and the focused energy you can devote to causes close to God's heart are all sacred gifts. As Paul notes in 1 Corinthians 7:32-34, those who are unmarried can concern themselves with the Lord's affairs and how to please Him with undivided devotion.

Consider these pathways to meaningful service:

- **Identify Your Divine Assignment:** Through prayer and spiritual discernment, seek where God is specifically calling you to serve. Sometimes the greatest impact comes from saying 'yes' to the small, consistent acts of service He places before you.
- **Leverage Your Unique Gifts:** God has purposefully equipped you with specific talents and experiences. How might these gifts meet the needs in your community or church family?
- **Build Sustainable Service Rhythms:** Create regular patterns of service that can be maintained long-term without leading to burnout. Remember, Jesus often

withdrew to quiet places even amid His ministry (Luke 5:16).

One beautiful aspect of service is how it connects us deeply with others while addressing our own need for community and purpose. When we serve, we often find ourselves being served through the relationships and experiences God orchestrates. As Proverbs 11:25 reminds us, *"Whoever refreshes others will be refreshed."*

Perhaps you're wondering how to begin this journey of meaningful service. Start with these prayerful steps:

- Ask the Holy Spirit to open your eyes to needs around you that align with your gifts and calling.
- Seek counsel from spiritual mentors who can help discern where your service might be most effective.
- Start small but remain consistent, allowing God to expand your impact in His timing.

Your service matters—not because it fills time or makes up for being single, but because it fulfills God's purpose for your life. Every act of service—whether visiting an elderly neighbor, mentoring a young believer, or volunteering at a local food bank—is part of God's beautiful tapestry of redemption.

The world may measure impact through numbers and recognition, but God sees every quiet act done in love. As Jesus said, even a simple cup of cold water given in His name carries eternal significance (Matthew 10:42). When your service flows from a heart aligned with His purpose, nothing you do is ever small in His eyes.

As you navigate this path of service, hold these truths close:

- Your service is an expression of worship, not a search for worth.
- Impact often happens in the quiet, unseen moments of faithfulness.
- God multiplies our offerings when surrendered to His purposes.

Let us pray together:

"Heavenly Father, show us how to use this season of singleness to serve others with Your love. Guide us to opportunities where our gifts can meet real needs. Help us maintain balance and joy in our service, remembering that we serve from Your strength, not our own. In Jesus' name, Amen."

Your journey of service may not always follow a straight path, but trust that God is using every step to create impact that reaches far beyond what you can see today. As you continue to serve faithfully, may you experience the deep joy that comes from living a life aligned with His purposes.

As we conclude this pivotal chapter on building a purposeful career and creating meaningful impact, let's pause to reflect on the transformative journey we've explored together. We've discovered that our professional paths aren't merely about climbing corporate ladders or achieving worldly success—they're about aligning our work with God's divine purposes for our lives. Through Aurora's story and the practical strategies we've discussed, we've seen how our single season provides unique advantages for career development and kingdom impact.

We've learned that titles or achievements don't measure true success, but by how faithfully we steward the gifts and opportunities God has entrusted to us. The flexibility and focus available in our single season create unprecedented opportunities to pursue excellence while maintaining spiritual integrity. As Colossians 3:23 reminds us, "Whatever you do, work at it with all your heart, as working for the Lord, not for human masters."

Action Steps:

- Schedule regular time for prayer about your career direction.
- Create a personal mission statement that integrates your professional goals with spiritual purpose.
- Identify one way to increase your kingdom impact in your current workplace this week.
- Seek mentorship from spiritually mature professionals in your field.

Key Chapter Takeaways:

- Your career is a platform for ministry and impact, not just a means of earning.
- The single season provides unique advantages for career development and purpose alignment.
- True success combines professional excellence with kingdom impact.
- Your work can become worship when aligned with God's purposes.

Reflection Questions:

- How am I currently using my professional platform for kingdom impact?

- What steps can I take to better align my career goals with God's purposes?
- Where do I see opportunities for greater service through my work?
    - How can I better steward the gifts God has given me in my current role?

Scriptures for Meditation:

- "Commit to the Lord whatever you do, and he will establish your plans." (Proverbs 16:3)
- "For we are God's handiwork, created in Christ Jesus to do good works, which God prepared in advance for us to do." (Ephesians 2:10)
- "Many are the plans in a person's heart, but it is the Lord's purpose that prevails." (Proverbs 19:21)

Beloved, as you move forward from this chapter, remember that your work isn't separate from your calling—it's an integral part of your divine purpose. Your single season provides precious opportunities to develop professionally while creating meaningful impact. Don't wait for some future season to begin living purposefully—start today, right where you are.

The journey of aligning your career with kingdom purpose is ongoing, but each step taken in faith moves you closer to fulfilling God's unique plan for your life. As you implement the strategies and principles we've explored, trust that God is faithful to guide your path and establish the work of your hands.

Remember, you're not just building a career—you're creating a legacy of impact that extends far beyond your professional achievements. Embrace this season with confidence, knowing that God has equipped you for every good work He has prepared for you to do.

Prayer focus:

Let's close with this powerful truth from Jeremiah 29:11: "For I know the plans I have for you," declares the Lord, "plans to prosper you and not to harm you, plans to give you hope and a future." Your career journey is part of God's greater plan for your life. Trust His timing, follow His leading, and watch how He uses your professional path for His glory.

Dear Father, guide me as I seek to honor You through my work. Help me see my careers through Your eyes and use my professional influence for Your kingdom. Give me wisdom in making career decisions and courage to follow Your leading, even when it differs from worldly wisdom, in Jesus' name, Amen.

Chapter 6

Boundaries and Blessings: Navigating Family and Social Expectations

"Then you will know the truth, and the truth will set you free."

Setting healthy boundaries can feel like walking a tightrope, especially when it involves family relationships and social expectations as a single adult. Our hearts long to honor our families and keep the peace, yet we must also protect our own sense of purpose and emotional well-being. The pressure to meet others' expectations or follow their timelines can be overwhelming, but it's in finding this balance that we discover the beauty of authentic living grounded in biblical truth. In a world that often pushes singles to compromise their values or rush into relationships, learning to establish healthy boundaries becomes not just important but essential for spiritual and emotional well-being. As Proverbs 4:23 reminds us, *"Above all else, guard your heart, for everything you do flows from it."* This divine wisdom perfectly captures why boundary-setting isn't just a modern self-help concept but a biblical principle for protecting our peace and purpose.

Navigating family dynamics requires particular wisdom and grace. While Scripture calls us to honor our parents (Exodus

20:12), it also acknowledges the importance of establishing healthy adult relationships (Genesis 2:24). This balance becomes especially crucial for singles facing well-meaning but sometimes overwhelming family involvement in their personal lives.[32]

Skylar's story powerfully illustrates this journey. At 37, she found herself dreading family gatherings, where well-intentioned relatives would inevitably steer conversations toward her relationship status. Each Sunday dinner became an exercise in polite deflection, with her aunt's matchmaking attempts and her mother's not-so-subtle hints about grandchildren leaving her emotionally drained.

This chapter will explore practical strategies for establishing healthy boundaries while maintaining loving relationships. We'll discuss how to communicate your needs effectively, manage social expectations without compromising your values, and find the delicate balance between honoring family relationships and staying true to your God-given purpose.

Through biblical wisdom and practical application, you'll discover that setting boundaries isn't about building walls—it's about creating healthy spaces where relationships can flourish while maintaining personal integrity. It's about learning to say "no" to what doesn't align with your values while saying "yes" to what nurtures your spiritual growth and purpose.

The journey to establishing healthy boundaries is ultimately about finding freedom—freedom to live authentically, pursue God's purpose, and maintain meaningful relationships without compromising your values or peace. As Jesus said in John 8:32, "Then you will know the truth, and the truth will set you free." It is getting freedom in truth.

As we journey through this chapter together, you'll find tools for navigating common challenges, scriptural foundations for boundary-setting, and encouragement for walking this path with grace and confidence. Establishing healthy boundaries isn't just about protecting yourself; it's about creating the space needed to live authentically and purposefully in your current season.

Setting Biblical Boundaries Without Guilt: Understanding God's Design for Healthy Relationships

Understanding God's design for healthy relationships begins with recognizing that boundaries are not barriers but divine guidelines for flourishing relationships. As we explore this crucial aspect of single living, we'll discover how setting biblical boundaries actually enhances our connections while protecting our God-given purpose and peace.

The journey to setting healthy boundaries often begins with a moment of clarity—a realization that current patterns aren't serving God's best for our lives or relationships. For Skylar, that moment came during a particularly challenging Sunday family dinner. As she sat at her parents' mahogany dining table, surrounded by the familiar faces of loved ones, her aunt Maria enthusiastically pulled out her phone.

"Look who I met at church today!" her aunt exclaimed, sliding the device across the table. "He's a young doctor; he just finished his residency. Such a nice Christian boy!" Skylar felt her chest tighten as she forced another polite smile, the same one she'd worn through countless similar scenarios.

For months, Skylar had been struggling with these well-intentioned but overwhelming attempts to guide her love life. Each family gathering had become a subtle reminder of what her relatives perceived as her 'incomplete' status. Despite her flourishing career as a youth counsellor and her active ministry involvement, conversations inevitably circled back to her singleness.

After much prayer and counsel from her mentor, Sarah, Skylar realized that avoiding confrontation wasn't protecting relationships—it was preventing authentic connection. Drawing strength from Scripture, particularly Proverbs 4:23's wisdom about guarding one's heart, she decided to approach the situation with both truth and grace.

The following Sunday, when her mother began her usual subtle hints about grandchildren, Skylar took a deep breath and spoke up. "Mom, Aunt Maria, everyone—I need to share something important," she began, her voice gentle but firm. "I know your suggestions and concern come from a place of love, but when every conversation focuses on my relationship status, it makes me feel like who I am right now isn't enough."

She continued, carefully choosing her words: "God has given me incredible opportunities to impact young lives through counseling and ministry. I'm not putting my life on hold waiting for marriage—I'm actively living the purpose He's given me right now. I would love for our family time to be about sharing these current blessings rather than constantly focusing on what's missing."

The silence that followed felt eternal. Then, unexpectedly, her mother's eyes welled with tears. "Oh, sweetheart," she said, reaching for Skylar's hand. "I never meant to make you feel less valued. I just worry about your happiness."

"I know, Mom," Skylar replied softly. "But my happiness isn't determined by my relationship status. It's found in pursuing God's purpose for my life."

Aunt Maria set down her phone, her expression thoughtful. "I never considered how my matchmaking might affect you," she admitted. "I guess I was so focused on what I thought you needed, I wasn't seeing what God was already doing in your life."

This honest conversation marked a turning point. Over the following months, family gatherings underwent significant changes. Instead of scrutinizing her single status, relatives began asking about her counselling ministry and the youth retreat she was organizing. Her mother even joined her for a volunteer day at the crisis center where Skylar worked.

The boundaries Skylar established didn't distance her from family—they created space for more authentic relationships to flourish. Her courage to speak truth in love allowed others to see her complete in Christ, not lacking or waiting to begin real life.

Her story illustrates a crucial truth: biblical boundaries aren't walls that separate us from loved ones but bridge the gap between false expectations and authentic relationships. They're founded on the understanding that our worth isn't determined by relationship status but by our identity in Christ. When we establish boundaries with grace and truth, we create space for genuine connection while honoring God's design for our lives.

We may love others more by being open and honest about our needs and limitations, as these boundaries are based on Scripture rather than selfishness.³³ While remaining faithful to our God-given assignment and calling, they help us maintain wholesome relationships.

Setting boundaries isn't about controlling others or shoving them away; rather, it's about making room for sincere connections to flourish while staying true to God's plan for our lives, as seen by Skylar's path. When we establish boundaries with love, wisdom, and prayer, we often find that the very relationships we were afraid of losing become stronger as a result of open communication and mutual respect.

Although setting boundaries can be difficult for many single people, especially when dealing with well-meaning family members or church members. Jesus Himself set an example of setting boundaries guilt-free by politely denying inappropriate demands (John 7:6) and frequently leaving crowds to pray (Luke 5:16). This shows us that setting limits is not only acceptable but also essential for maintaining spiritual well-being.

Managing Family Dynamics: Balancing Honor with Personal Space

When it comes to navigating family dynamics and social expectations as a single adult, many find themselves caught in an intricate dance of honoring relationships while maintaining personal boundaries. The pressure to conform to others' timelines and expectations can feel overwhelming, yet it's within this delicate balance that we discover the beauty of authentic living rooted in biblical truth.

Scripture's definition of honor extends beyond simple compliance. It includes upholding sound boundaries and showing genuine concern, respect, and regard for family ties. According to the teachings of the apostle Paul, we should continue to honor our parents as adults (Ephesians 6:2-3), but we must balance this with our primary loyalty to God and His plan for our lives.

Creating and keeping one's personal space is not selfish; rather, it is necessary for one's emotional and spiritual well-being. To fulfill His heavenly mission, Jesus occasionally withdrew from family distractions (Luke 2:49). We can learn from this that God's creation includes room for spiritual and personal development.

Many singles face intense cultural pressure regarding marriage and family involvement. Your journey may require wisdom in navigating between cultural expectations and personal convictions. Building strong family relationships is built on understanding, clear communication, and mutual respect. As Proverbs 24:3-4 teaches, "By wisdom a house is built, and through understanding it is established; through knowledge its rooms are filled with rare and beautiful treasures."

Practical Steps for Balancing Family Dynamics

- Establish Clear Communication Channels
- Express appreciation for family concern
- Share your perspective with gentleness.
- Set expectations about availability and involvement

Maintain Consistent Boundaries

- Respond to pressure with grace and firmness
- Honor family traditions while protecting personal values
- Practice saying "no" when necessary

Action Steps for Implementation

- Self-Assessment
- Evaluate and understand the current family dynamics
- Identify areas that need boundaries
- List specific areas you need to take action for improvement.

Communication Planning

- Prepare respectful responses to common situations
- Practice expressing needs clearly
- Develop strategies for handling difficult conversations

Support Building

- Identify positive influences in your life
- Connect and relate with like-minded individuals
- Establish regular encouragement routines

A healthy rhythm that respects both family and personal space is the key to regulating family dynamics, so keep that in mind. Trust God to lead you in creating relationships that are a reflection of His knowledge and love as you put these ideas into practice.

Responding to Social Pressure: Maintaining Grace Under Scrutiny

The constant scrutiny and pressure that singles face can feel like waves testing the shores of their resolve. Yet, like a lighthouse standing firm through storms, maintaining grace under this pressure isn't just possible—it's transformative. These influences from society frequently manifest as well-intentioned but unwanted requests, inappropriate advice, or subconscious cues that something is lacking in our lives. Maintaining grace under scrutiny requires both inner strength and wisdom (John 8:15-16). This delicate balance becomes especially crucial for singles navigating a world that often misunderstands or diminishes the value of unmarried life. Developing a solid relationship with oneself is crucial for both individual fulfillment and wholesome interpersonal interactions. This relationship with oneself becomes important when one is subject to social criticism.

If left unchecked, these pressures can lead to self-doubt and erode one's sense of self-worth. But according to Scripture, God determines our value, not our relationship status or social expectations (1 Samuel 16:7).

Social pressure, while challenging, can become a catalyst for deeper spiritual growth and stronger character. As Romans 5:3-4 reminds us, "We also glory in our sufferings, because we know that suffering produces perseverance; perseverance, character; and character, hope."

The journey of maintaining grace under scrutiny isn't about perfection but progression. Every encounter becomes an opportunity to demonstrate the love of Christ while remaining true to your God-given identity and destiny.[34] Like Skylar discovered, when we respond to pressure with grace-filled truth, we often find that the very relationships we feared damaging actually grow stronger through honest communication and mutual respect.

Responding with grace doesn't mean passive acceptance of every opinion or suggestion. Instead, it means choosing to see beyond the pressure to the hearts of those who care about us, while firmly standing in the truth of who God has called us to be in this season. This balance of grace and truth not only preserves our peace but also often opens doors for deeper, more authentic relationships built on mutual understanding and respect.

Throughout this chapter, we've witnessed, through Skylar's story, how speaking the truth in love can transform challenging family dynamics into opportunities for deeper connection.

Skylar's journey from dreading family gatherings to experiencing genuine fellowship reminds us that authentic relationships flourish when we courageously establish loving boundaries. Her story illustrates three fundamental truths about sacred boundaries:

- Boundaries aren't walls that separate us but bridges that connect us more authentically.
- Speaking truth in love can strengthen rather than damage relationships.
- Honoring family doesn't require compromising God's purpose for your life.

Action Steps:

Identify one boundary you need to establish or strengthen.

- Write out your loving but firm response to common pressure points.
- Schedule intentional conversations with family members about your needs
- Create a support system to help you maintain healthy boundaries.
- Journal about your boundary-setting journey and God's faithfulness in the process

Key Chapter Takeaway:

Let's reflect on the practical wisdom we've gained:

- Sacred Response Strategy
- Prepare thoughtful, grace-filled responses to common pressure points
- Address concerns with gentle firmness rather than defensive reactions.
- Keep the focus on God's current work in your life.
- Express appreciation for others' concern while establishing clear boundaries

Reflection Questions:

- How have your current boundaries (or lack thereof) affected your family relationships?
- What specific conversations do you need to have with loved ones about boundaries?
- How can you better honor both God and family through your boundary-setting?
- What new patterns of interaction do you need to establish?

Scriptures for Meditation:

- Proverbs 4:23—"Above all else, guard your heart, for everything you do flows from it."
- Matthew 5:37—"Let your 'Yes' be 'Yes,' and your 'No,' 'No.'"
- Ephesians 6:2–3—"Honor your father and mother... that it may go well with you."
- Galatians 1:10—"Am I now trying to win the approval of human beings, or of God?"

Prayer Focus:

Heavenly Father, grant me wisdom to establish boundaries that honor You while maintaining loving relationships with others. Help me respond with grace under pressure and stay true to the purpose You've given me. Guide me in creating spaces where genuine love and respect can flourish. In Jesus' name, amen.

Chapter 7

Financial Freedom: Creating Stability and Success as a Single

"Wealth gained hastily will dwindle, but whoever gathers little by little will increase it."

The journey to financial freedom begins with a single step of courage and conviction. As a single person, you have the unique advantage of complete autonomy over your financial decisions, an opportunity that, when wisely stewarded, can become your greatest asset in building lasting wealth. In a world where financial independence can feel both liberating and daunting, understanding God's principles for monetary stewardship becomes essential for creating lasting stability and success. This chapter will guide you through biblical wisdom and practical strategies for building wealth, managing resources, and developing long-term financial security as a single person.

Consider Florence's story. She sat at her kitchen table, surrounded by bills and bank statements, feeling overwhelmed by the responsibility of managing her finances alone. As a successful marketing professional, she earned a decent income but struggled with the pressure of being the sole provider for herself. One evening, after a particularly challenging day at work, she decided to take control of her financial future. She began by creating a detailed budget and setting aside 20% of her income for savings and investments. Within six months, Florence had paid off her credit card debt and started building an emergency fund. But her true breakthrough came when she realized that there's more to financial freedom than just about having more money—it's also about stewardship and purpose. She began viewing her resources through a biblical lens, understanding that everything she had was a gift from God to be managed wisely. This shift in perspective led her to start a small side business offering marketing consulting services to local nonprofits, allowing her to increase her income while making a meaningful impact in her community. Two years later, Florence had not only achieved her financial goals but had also become a mentor to other singles around her, teaching them the principles of biblical financial management.

Florence's journey mirrors what many singles face—the challenge of building financial stability while honoring God's principles of stewardship. The good news is that your single season presents unique opportunities for financial growth and impact. Without the immediate responsibilities of providing for a family, you have the freedom to make strategic financial decisions that can set a strong foundation for your future.

In this chapter, we'll explore God's perspective on prosperity (3 John 1:2), examine practical strategies for wealth building, and discover how to create multiple streams of income. We'll address common financial challenges singles face and provide biblical solutions for overcoming them. Most importantly, we'll learn how to view our resources through the lens of stewardship, understanding that financial freedom isn't just about personal security—it's about positioning ourselves to be a blessing to others and advance God's kingdom.

As we discuss these principles, remember that God's promise in Proverbs 10:22 states, *"The blessing of the LORD makes one rich, and He adds no sorrow with it."* This chapter will equip you with both spiritual wisdom and practical tools to step into the financial freedom God intends for you.

Biblical Stewardship: Understanding God's Principles for Financial Management

The foundation of financial freedom begins with a profound truth: everything belongs to God.[35] As Psalm 24:1 declares, *"The earth is the Lord's, and everything in it, the world, and all who live in it."* This revolutionary perspective transforms our approach to money management from mere personal responsibility into sacred stewardship.

Key Principle: We Are Managers, Not Owners

When we grasp that we're managing God's resources rather than our own, and we must give an account of how we manage them, it fundamentally shifts how we:

- Make financial decisions
- View wealth accumulation
- Approach giving and generosity
- Plan for the future

As singles, we have a unique opportunity to establish strong financial foundations based on biblical principles. Rather than viewing this season as one of limited resources or waiting for shared financial responsibility, we can embrace it as a period of focused stewardship and intentional wealth building.[36]

Three Pillars of Biblical Stewardship

- **Divine Ownership:** Recognising God's ultimate ownership of all resources
- **Faithful Management:** Developing systems for wise resource allocation
- **Kingdom Purpose:** Aligning financial decisions with God's priorities

Practical Application of Stewardship

Implementing biblical stewardship in daily life involves:

- Creating a budget that reflects God's priorities
- Practising the principle of first fruits giving, tithe, offering, and giving to the needy.
- Establishing emergency savings
- Developing multiple income streams through diligent work

Breaking Free from Financial Bondage

Proverbs 22:7 warns that "the borrower is servant to the lender." As singles, we have the unique opportunity to establish debt-free living early through:

- Strategic way for debt repayment
- Intentional in spending decisions
- Building emergency reserves
- Living below our income

The Power of Contentment

One of the most challenging aspects of financial stewardship is maintaining contentment while building wealth.[37] 1 Timothy 6:6 reminds us that "godliness with contentment is great gain." By keeping this equilibrium, we can avoid materialism and promote prudent resource management.

Wisdom for the Journey

Remember these key scriptural principles:

- "Honor the Lord with your wealth" (Proverbs 3:9)
- "The plans of the diligent lead surely to abundance" (Proverbs 21:5)
- "Where your treasure is, there your heart will be also" (Matthew 6:21)

You have exceptional chances to build a solid financial foundation during your single season. By putting these biblical stewardship principles into practice, you're doing more than just handling your finances; you're additionally letting God use your resources and getting ready for a bigger kingdom influence.

Recall that biblical stewardship is about freedom rather than limitation. God promises us peace and provision when we match our financial habits with His values. Your legacy and future influence are built on the financial choices you make today.

Strategic Wealth Building: Investment Strategies and Long-term Planning for Singles

Building wealth as a single person requires strategic planning and disciplined execution.[38] While the journey may seem daunting without a partner's financial support, your single season actually presents unique advantages for focused wealth building and investment growth. As Proverbs 21:5 reminds us, *"The plans of the diligent lead surely to abundance, but everyone who is hasty comes only to poverty."*

The Divine Perspective on Prosperity

The foundation of strategic wealth building begins with understanding that financial prosperity is part of God's plan for His children. 3 John 1:2 affirms, "Beloved, I pray that you may prosper in all things and be in health, just as your soul prospers." This prosperity isn't just about accumulation - it's about stewardship and kingdom impact.

Key Investment Strategies for Singles

- Maximize retirement contributions through employer plans and Individual Retirement Accounts (IRAs)
- Build a diverse investment portfolio across multiple asset classes
- Create multiple income streams through strategic side ventures
- Maintain comprehensive insurance coverage
- Establish clear estate planning documents

The Power of Independent Financial Decision-Making

One of your greatest advantages as a single person is the ability to make autonomous financial choices. This independence allows you to align investments precisely with your goals and risk tolerance. However, this freedom requires greater discipline and intentional planning.

Smart Automation: Your Silent Wealth Builder

Consistent, automated investing harnesses the power of compound interest, which Albert Einstein reportedly called the "eighth wonder of the world." By removing emotion from the equation through automation, you ensure steady progress toward your financial goals.

Building Your Wealth Streams

Ecclesiastes 11:2 provides timeless wisdom about diversification: *"Give a portion to seven, or even to eight, for you know not what disaster may happen on earth."* Consider developing:

1. Active Income Streams:

- Career advancement opportunities
- Consulting or freelance work
- Teaching or coaching in your area of expertise

2. Investment Income

- Stock market investments
- Real estate holdings
- Dividend-paying assets
- Interest-bearing accounts

3. Digital and Creative Assets

- Online businesses
- Digital products and courses
- Content creation
- Intellectual property

4. Service-Based Revenue

- Professional services
- Coaching programs
- Community workshops
- Specialized consulting

Biblical Wisdom for Wealth Building

Let these scriptures guide your financial journey:

- "Wealth gained hastily will dwindle, but whoever gathers little by little will increase it" (Proverbs 13:11)
- The Parable of the Talents (Matthew 25:14-30)
- "The blessing of the LORD makes rich, and He adds no sorrow with it" (Proverbs 10:22)

Building wealth as a single person isn't just about accumulating money; it's about creating a foundation for greater kingdom impact and service.[39] As you implement these strategies, focus on being a faithful steward of what God has entrusted to you, using your resources to bless others and advance His purposes.

Your single season provides a unique opportunity to lay a strong financial foundation.[40] By combining biblical wisdom with strategic planning, you can build lasting wealth that serves both your future and God's kingdom purposes.

Essential Protection Strategies

Proverbs 22:3 teaches, *"The prudent sees danger and hides himself, but the simple go on and suffer for it."* This divine wisdom underscores the importance of emergency preparedness, especially for singles who must create robust safety nets independently. Protect your growing wealth through:

Financial Safety Nets:

- Maintain 6-8 months of living expenses in emergency savings41
- Secure comprehensive insurance coverage
- Create clear estate planning documents
- Implement tax-efficient investment strategies

Reflection & Action Points

- Create an investment policy statement outlining your goals and strategies
- Establish automatic transfers to investment and savings accounts
- Research and implement one new income stream this quarter
- Review and update your estate planning documents annually
- Build relationships with trusted financial advisors who share your values

Essential Components of Emergency Readiness

Financial Foundation

- Emergency fund covering 6-8 months of expenses
- Readily accessible savings account
- Strategic cash reserves
- Regular financial reviews and adjustments

Emergency Resources Kit

- Essential supplies and necessities
- Important documents and records

- Medical supplies and prescriptions
- Basic survival items

Communication Protocol

- Emergency contact list
- Digital document backups
- Clear communication plan
- Support network activation system

Practical Implementation Steps

For Income Streams:

- Assess your current skills and resources
- Identify potential income opportunities
- Create an implementation timeline
- Set specific income goals
- Regularly evaluate and adjust strategies

For Emergency Preparedness:

- Build your emergency fund systematically
- Create and maintain your emergency kit42
- Document your emergency plan
- Practice your response protocols
- Review and update regularly

Success Mindset

Remember that financial independence isn't about hoarding wealth—it's about wise stewardship that enables us to live purposefully and serve others effectively. As Proverbs 13:11 teaches, *"Wealth gained hastily will dwindle, but whoever gathers little by little will increase it."*

Your single season offers a unique opportunity for focused financial growth and lasting impact. Without the immediate responsibility of providing for a family, you have the freedom to make wise, strategic choices that build a strong foundation for your future.[43] Remember Florence's story—how she moved from feeling overwhelmed by money to becoming a mentor who helps others understand biblical financial principles. Her journey shows that when we shift our focus from simply managing money to intentionally stewarding God's resources, we experience both personal prosperity and lasting kingdom impact. As we wrap up this chapter on financial freedom and stewardship, let's remember that our journey toward financial stability is both a practical endeavor and a spiritual calling. The principles we've explored form a comprehensive framework for creating lasting financial success as a single person.

Continue to seek God's wisdom in your financial decisions, trusting that He will guide you as you apply these principles. Remember, "For I know the plans I have for you, declares the LORD, plans to prosper you and not to harm you, plans to give you hope and a future" (Jeremiah 29:11). Let this promise encourage you as you pursue financial freedom with purpose and wisdom.

Action Steps:

- Create or update your monthly budget based on biblical principles
- Establish automatic savings for your emergency fund
- Identify and begin developing one new income stream
- Review and update your emergency preparedness plan
- Schedule your next financial review

Key Chapter Takeaway:

- Biblical stewardship as the foundation of financial wisdom
- Strategic wealth building through intentional planning
- Multiple income streams for financial resilience
- Emergency preparedness as an act of wisdom

Reflection Questions:

- How has your perspective on financial stewardship changed?
- What unique skills could become income streams?
- Where are the gaps in my emergency preparedness?
- What specific steps will you take this week to improve your financial management?
- How can you use your resources more effectively to bless others?

Scripture to Meditate on:

- "The blessing of the LORD makes one rich, and He adds no sorrow with it" (Proverbs 10:22)
- "For the LORD your God will bless you just as He promised you" (Deuteronomy 15:6)
- "Wealth gained hastily will dwindle, but whoever gathers little by little will increase it" (Proverbs 13:11)

Prayer Focus:

Heavenly Father, thank You for the principles of financial wisdom You've provided in Your Word. Help me to be a faithful steward of all You've entrusted to me. Grant me wisdom as I build financial independence and prepare for the future, and wisdom in managing resources, contentment in all circumstances, and a generous heart that reflects Your character. Guide my financial decisions and help me use my resources to bless others and advance Your kingdom. In Jesus' name, Amen.

Chapter 8

Community and Connection: Building Meaningful Relationships

"As iron sharpens iron, so one person sharpens another."

The myth that single life equals lonely life has persisted far too long in our society, casting unnecessary shadows over what can be one of the most relationally rich seasons of life. The truth is, our single season offers unique opportunities to cultivate deep, meaningful connections across multiple spheres of life; from family and friends to mentors and ministry partners. Like a tapestry woven with threads of different colors and textures, our lives are enriched by the diverse relationships we cultivate along our journey. In our fast-paced digital age, where connections often remain surface-level and transactional, the call to build deep, meaningful relationships becomes even more crucial for our spiritual and emotional well-being.

The scriptures remind us that we were created for community— "It is not good for man to be alone" (Genesis 2:18). This truth extends beyond romantic relationships to encompass the full spectrum of human connections that God intends for our lives. As single believers, we have the unique opportunity to invest deeply in various forms of relationships that can bring richness and purpose to our lives.

Building Bonds That Last

Meaningful relationships don't just happen—they require intentional cultivation, wisdom in choosing with whom to connect, and the courage to be vulnerable.[44] Proverbs 27:17 tells us that "as iron sharpens iron, so one person sharpens another." This scripture perfectly captures the transformative power of authentic relationships in our lives.

Willa's story serves as a powerful reminder of how self-sufficiency, while appearing to be a strength, can actually become a barrier to experiencing the fullness of community that God intends for us. Her journey from isolation to authentic connection mirrors the path many singles must navigate. When she faced job loss, her initial instinct to retreat reflected a common struggle—the fear that vulnerability equals weakness.

However, her experience beautifully illustrates the truth found in Ecclesiastes 4:9-10: "Two are better than one, because they have a good return for their labor: if either of them falls, one can help the other up."

Creating Spaces for Authentic Connection

Genuine community extends beyond casual friendships or social media connections. It involves creating environments where we can be fully known and fully accepted, where we can share our victories and vulnerabilities, and where we can grow together in faith and purpose. This kind of community requires stepping beyond our comfort zones and embracing the beautiful mess of real relationships.

Nurturing Different Types of Relationships

As singles, we have the unique opportunity to invest in various forms of meaningful connections:

- Mentoring relationships that provide wisdom and guidance
- Peer friendships that offer mutual support and understanding
- Family bonds that ground us in belonging
- Ministry partnerships that align with our purpose
- Professional networks that support our career growth

Each of these relationships serves a distinct purpose in our lives, contributing to our overall growth and well-being. When we actively cultivate these different types of connections, we create a rich tapestry of support that reflects God's design for community.

Breaking Free from Isolation

Isolation often whispers lies that keep us from reaching out—lies about self-sufficiency, about being a burden, or about not needing others. Yet Scripture consistently emphasizes the importance of community in our spiritual journey. Hebrews 10:24-25 encourages us to "consider how we may spur one another on toward love and good deeds, not giving up meeting together. Each relationship you nurture can become a channel for God's grace and purpose in your life, creating a legacy of love that extends far beyond your current season.

Cultivating Deep Friendships: Moving Beyond Surface-Level Connections

In a world increasingly connected yet paradoxically isolated, the art of cultivating deep friendships becomes not just a social nicety but a vital spiritual discipline. As Proverbs 18:24 reminds us, "One who has unreliable friends soon comes to ruin, but there is a friend who sticks closer than a brother." This scripture illuminates the profound difference between having many acquaintances and nurturing true, life-giving friendships.

The journey from surface-level connections to meaningful friendships requires intentional effort and divine wisdom.[45] Sarah was a successful executive who found herself surrounded by professional networks yet yearning for deeper connections. Through deliberate steps of vulnerability and commitment, she transformed casual coffee meetings into spaces for authentic sharing and spiritual growth. Her story exemplifies how intentional friendship cultivation can revolutionize our single season.

Practical steps for deepening friendships often begin with small, consistent actions:

- Schedule regular, uninterrupted time for meaningful conversation
- Practice active listening without rushing to offer solutions
- Share beyond surface-level topics, including struggles and victories
- Create shared experiences that build lasting memories
- Establish regular prayer partnerships or accountability relationships

The cultivation of deep friendships also requires wisdom in navigating potential challenges. Many singles face the temptation to withdraw when friends enter different life stages or when vulnerability feels risky. However, these moments often present opportunities for relationship growth rather than reasons for retreat. James 1:19 offers timeless guidance: "Everyone should be quick to listen, slow to speak, and slow to become angry," providing a foundation for navigating friendship transitions with grace.

Creating spaces for authentic connection involves more than just social gathering—it requires intentional cultivation of environments where truth can be spoken in love (Ephesians 4:15). This might look like:

- Hosting regular dinner gatherings focused on meaningful conversation
- Joining or starting a small group centered on shared interests and spiritual growth
- Establishing regular check-ins with trusted friends for mutual encouragement[50]
- Creating opportunities for serving together in ministry or community service

The depth of our friendships often reflects our willingness to be known. Consider establishing what I call "Friendship Rhythms"—regular practices that create space for deepening relationships:

- Monthly one-on-one coffee dates focused on heart-level conversations
- Quarterly adventure days that create shared experiences and memories

- Annual retreats or planning sessions to reflect on life goals and spiritual growth
- Weekly prayer partnerships that foster spiritual intimacy and accountability

Deep friendships don't develop overnight—they require patience, intentionality, and consistent investment. As Ecclesiastes 4:9-10 teaches, this mutual support system becomes particularly vital during challenging seasons of life.

Practical Application Steps:

- Identify three friendships you want to deepen this month.
- Schedule regular, intentional time for meaningful conversation.
- Create a list of questions that move beyond surface-level chat.
- Establish a friendship ritual or tradition.
- Practice vulnerability by sharing something personal.

As you implement these strategies, remember that authentic friendship-building is both an art and a spiritual practice. It requires discernment, patience, and trust in God's timing. Your investment in deep friendships today creates a foundation of support and community that will enrich every season of your life.

Reflection Questions:

- How am I currently investing in my friendships?
- What barriers am I maintaining that prevent deeper connections?
- Where might God be calling me to greater vulnerability in my relationships?

- How can I create more intentional spaces for meaningful connection?

Through intentional cultivation of deep friendships, we create communities that reflect God's heart for connection and support our growth in this season of life. These relationships become not just social connections but vital channels through which God's grace, wisdom, and love flow in our lives.

Building a Support System: The Power of Intentional Community

Living as a single adult offers unique opportunities to build rich, meaningful connections that can transform our journey from merely surviving to genuinely thriving.[46] While modern culture often equates singleness with isolation, Scripture paints a different picture—one of purposeful community and intentional relationships that strengthen our faith and purpose.

The apostle Paul's ministry provides a powerful model of intentional community. Throughout his letters, we see evidence of deep, purposeful relationships that sustained his mission—from Timothy, whom he mentored, to Priscilla and Aquila, who risked their lives for him (Romans 16:3-4). This biblical example shows us that building strong support systems isn't just about having people around—it's about cultivating relationships that align with our values and contribute to our spiritual growth.

Singles who actively build support systems experience greater emotional resilience and life satisfaction. However, creating these networks requires intentional effort and wisdom. Consider these biblical principles as you build your community:

- Seek wisdom in choosing connections (Proverbs 13:20).

- Invest in authentic relationships (1 Thessalonians 2:8).
- Create regular rhythms of connection (Hebrews 10:24-25)
- Practice vulnerability with trusted friends (James 5:16)
- Serve others within your community (1 Peter 4:10)

Galatians 6:2 instructs us to "Carry each other's burdens, and in this way you will fulfill the law of Christ." This scripture emphasizes the reciprocal nature of healthy community—both giving and receiving support. Your support system might include:

- Spiritual accountability partners who encourage growth in faith
- Practical support for daily life challenges
- Emotional confidants who provide safe spaces for vulnerability
- Mentors who offer wisdom and guidance
- Service relationships that allow us to give back

To overcome common barriers in building community, consider these practical steps:

- Schedule regular check-ins with key supporters.
- Join or create small groups focused on shared interests.
- Use technology thoughtfully to maintain connections
- Practice asking for help when needed.
- Commit to showing up consistently for others

Maintaining a strong support system requires ongoing investment. Romans 12:10 encourages us to "Be devoted to one another in love. Honor one another above yourselves." This principle guides us in nurturing lasting connections.

Building a strong support system isn't just about meeting our own needs—it's about creating spaces where God's love can flow through us to others. As we intentionally cultivate community, we participate in His design for human flourishing and find greater wholeness in our single season. Through these connections, we experience the truth of Ecclesiastes 4:12: *"Though one may be overpowered, two can defend themselves. A cord of three strands is not quickly broken."*

Maintaining Healthy Boundaries: Balancing Independence and Interdependence

The art of maintaining healthy boundaries lies at the heart of thriving relationships. Like a well-tended garden, these boundaries require wisdom to know what to nurture and what to prune. As singles, we have the unique opportunity to establish these parameters thoughtfully, creating spaces that honor both our independence and our need for meaningful connection.

Scripture provides profound wisdom for this balance. Jesus Himself modeled healthy boundaries—knowing when to engage with crowds and when to withdraw for solitude (Mark 1:35). His example reminds us that setting limits isn't selfish; it's a vital part of spiritual and emotional health. Healthy boundaries emerge from three essential foundations:

- Clear understanding of our values and non-negotiables
- Graceful yet firm communication of our needs
- Consistent maintenance of established limits

As Proverbs 4:23 instructs, "Guard your heart above all else, for it determines the course of your life." This principle guides us in protecting our emotional and spiritual wholeness while remaining open to authentic connection.

Healthy boundaries allow us to give and receive love freely, without losing our sense of identity or peace. They protect what God is cultivating within us while ensuring our relationships remain life-giving and rooted in grace.

Practical steps for maintaining this sacred balance include:

- Regular assessment of relationship dynamics
- Intentional time management between solitude and community
- Clear communication of expectations
- Recognition and respect for personal limits

When establishing boundaries, grace becomes our guide. Consider these approaches:

- Express limits with kindness and clarity.
- Acknowledge others' perspectives while holding firm to your values.
- Offer explanations when appropriate, without feeling obligated to justify every boundary.
- Make room for flexibility while maintaining core principles.

In our hyper-connected world, boundary-setting often faces unique challenges. Social media, instant messaging, and constant availability can blur the lines between healthy connection and overwhelming obligation.

Consider implementing what I call "Sacred Spaces"—designated times and places where you intentionally disconnect to reconnect with yourself and God.

Selective vulnerability plays a crucial role in boundary maintenance. Think of it as having different levels of access in your life—not everyone needs complete access to every area. This discernment allows for deep connection with trusted individuals while maintaining appropriate boundaries with others.

Healthy boundaries aren't walls but filters—they let in what nourishes and protect against what depletes. They create the conditions for authentic relationships to flourish while preserving your sense of self.

Reflection Exercise:

Consider these questions in your journal:

- Where do I need stronger boundaries in my relationships?
- How can I communicate my limits more effectively?
- What relationships energize me, and which ones deplete me?
- How can I better honor both my need for connection and solitude?

Practical Application:

- Create a "boundary blueprint"—identify your non-negotiables.
- Practice saying no to one request this week that doesn't align with your values.
- Schedule regular solitude for spiritual renewal.
- Identify relationships that need boundary adjustments.

As you implement these principles, remember that boundary-setting is both an act of self-care and neighbor love. It creates the space needed for authentic relationships to thrive while honoring your God-given need for personal space and spiritual renewal. Your boundaries become the foundation upon which meaningful connections can be built—not barriers to relationships, but bridges to a deeper, more sustainable community.

This chapter has exposed you to how to build meaningful relationships and create an authentic community. Focus on the practical steps that transform surface-level connections into deep, lasting bonds. The journey from isolation to vibrant community isn't about waiting for relationships to happen—it's about intentionally cultivating connections that reflect God's design for our lives.

Through Willa's story, we've witnessed how releasing the grip of self-sufficiency opens doors to experiencing the richness of genuine community. Her transformation reminds us that strength isn't found in isolation but in the courage to connect authentically with others. As Ecclesiastes 4:9-10 affirms, "Two are better than one, because they have a good return for their labor: If either of them falls, one can help the other up."

We've explored three essential components of building meaningful relationships:

- Moving beyond surface-level connections to cultivate deep friendships
- Creating intentional support systems that sustain us through every season
- Maintaining healthy boundaries that enable authentic connection

These elements work together to create relationships that enrich our lives and further God's purpose through us. The practical tools and biblical principles we've discussed provide a roadmap for transforming our community approach.

Action Steps:

- Identify one relationship to intentionally deepen this month
- Schedule regular, uninterrupted time for meaningful conversations.
- Create or join a small group focused on shared interests and spiritual growth.
- Practice vulnerability by sharing something meaningful with a trusted friend
- Establish connection rhythms that foster deeper relationships
- Implement healthy boundaries that protect while enabling authentic connection.
- Look for opportunities to serve within your community

Key Chapter Takeaway:

- Intentional cultivation and the willingness to be vulnerable are necessary for an authentic community
- Healthy boundaries facilitate rather than obstruct deeper connections
- Support networks are critical to thriving in this special season.
- The well-being of our community is influenced by each of us as individuals.

Reflection Questions:

- Which relationship-building strategy resonated most deeply with you?

- What specific steps will you take this week to deepen one key relationship?
- How can you create more intentional spaces for authentic connection?
- Where might God be calling you to greater vulnerability in community?

Scriptures to Meditate On:

- Ecclesiastes 4:9-10: "Two are better than one... If either of them falls, one can help the other up."
- Proverbs 27:17: "As iron sharpens iron, so one person sharpens another."
- Hebrews 10:24-25: "And let us consider how we may spur one another on toward love and good deeds, not giving up meeting together."

Building meaningful relationships is both an art and a spiritual practice. It requires patience, intentionality, and trust in God's timing. The connections you cultivate today create ripples of impact that extend far beyond your current season.

As you move forward, may you be encouraged by Paul's words in 1 Thessalonians 5:11: "Therefore encourage one another and build each other up, just as in fact you are doing." Your investment in authentic community isn't just about enriching your own life—it's about creating spaces where God's love can flow freely through meaningful connections.

Let this truth guide your steps as you continue building relationships that honor both your independence and your need for community. The friendships you nurture today are creating a legacy of love that will bear fruit for generations to come.

Prayer Focus:

Father, thank you for the community you have provided for us. Help us to relate well and set boundaries with wisdom so we can have a good relationship with people and the community around us. We trust You will lead us to the right people and community at the right time as we navigate through this journey in Jesus' name, amen.

Chapter 9

Healing and Hope: Processing Past Relationships with Grace

"A bruised reed he will not break, and a smouldering wick he will not snuff out."

Carrying the weight of past relationships can feel like lugging around stones in a backpack - each disappointment, heartbreak, and unmet expectation adding to the burden until moving forward becomes increasingly tough. Yet, within the gentle hands of Jesus Christ, these very stones that once weighed us down can become stepping stones towards healing and transformation. Matthew 11:28 says, 'Come to me, all who labour and are heavy laden, and I will give you rest.' Like the faithful hands of a potter reshaping clay, God's healing touch can transform our past relationship experiences into vessels of wisdom and grace. This chapter explores the delicate journey of processing past relationships while keeping an open heart for future possibilities - all through the lens of God's redemptive love.

Maybe you've found yourself, like Ruby in our opening story, sifting through the remnants of past relationships, wondering how to make sense of the hurt while holding onto hope. Ruby sat in her garden one Sunday afternoon, tears streaming down her face as she read through old journal entries documenting her three-year relationship with James. The relationship had ended six months ago, but the pain still felt raw. As she turned each page, she realised how much of herself she had lost trying to make the relationship work - compromising her values, dismissing red flags, and slowly disconnecting from her faith community.

The pain of past relationships can feel overwhelming. Yet, Scripture reminds us that God is "near to the brokenhearted and saves the crushed in spirit" (Psalm 34:18). In His divine economy, no experience is wasted; even our deepest hurts can become stepping stones towards wholeness and wisdom. Ruby's journey illustrates this truth as she chose to approach her healing intentionally through prayer, counselling, and honest conversations with trusted friends.

The journey of healing is both deeply personal and profoundly spiritual. While the world often encourages us to "just move on" or "get back out there," God's approach to healing is far more intentional and transformative. He invites us to bring our wounded hearts to Him, promising that He makes "all things new" (Revelation 21:5). This renewal isn't just about forgetting the past; it's about allowing God to redeem it.

Through biblical counselling, Ruby discovered how her fear of abandonment had led her to accept less than God's best for her life. Her story demonstrates how pain can become a catalyst for growth when surrendered to God's transformative power. A year later, Ruby looked back at her journal entries with different eyes, where she once saw only pain, she now saw growth; where she once saw failure, she now saw learning opportunities.

As we navigate this healing journey together, we'll explore practical tools and biblical principles for processing emotional wounds with grace, establishing healthy boundaries while keeping our hearts open, recognising and breaking unhealthy relationship patterns, and finding purpose in our pain. Remember, healing isn't just about getting over someone - it's about becoming whole in Christ.

As 2 Corinthians 5:17 reminds us, *"Therefore, if anyone is in Christ, the new creation has come: The old has gone, the new is here!"* This promise of renewal extends to every aspect of our lives, including our relationship experiences. Together, we'll discover how God can use our past relationships as building blocks for a stronger future—not despite our experiences, but because of how He redeems them.

Embracing God's Healing Grace: Moving from Hurt to Wholeness

Former relationships can leave us carrying emotional baggage - each disappointment, betrayal, and unmet expectation adding weight until moving forward feels impossible.[47] Yet in the gentle hands of our Saviour, these very stones that once weighed us down can become stepping stones towards healing and transformation. As Jesus invites us to "Come and He will give you rest.

Grace is more than just a spiritual concept; it's the active power of God working to bring restoration and renewal to our wounded hearts. When we've experienced relationship pain, this grace becomes our foundation for healing. As Paul reminds us in 2 Corinthians 12:9, "My grace is sufficient for you, for my power is made perfect in weakness." This promise assures us that even in our most vulnerable moments, God's grace is enough.

The journey from hurt to wholeness requires both receiving divine grace and extending grace to ourselves. As Lane Moore wisely counsels, "Just be gentler with yourself than you'd think you'd need to be. You already survived everything you survived." This aligns perfectly with God's gentle approach to our healing process as described in Isaiah 42:3, "A bruised reed he will not break, and a smouldering wick he will not snuff out."

Healing involves honest reflection while avoiding self-condemnation. John Kim's concept of radical acceptance becomes transformative when coupled with biblical truth - accepting our current season while trusting God's perfect timing and purpose. This means acknowledging pain while believing that healing is possible, knowing that wholeness comes not from relationship status but from inner transformation through Christ.

Practical steps in this healing journey include creating daily moments for prayer and reflection, processing emotions through journaling, and building a strong support system of faith-filled friends and mentors. It's also vital to establish healthy boundaries that protect your healing process while remaining open to what God has ahead.

True healing means embracing our complete identity in Christ. This truth becomes our foundation for moving forward with hope and purpose. Each day presents an opportunity to declare God's truth over our lives, engage in activities that nurture spiritual and emotional growth, and trust that He is working all things together for our good.

Healing is both a journey and a destination. Some days may feel like steps backward, but God's grace meets us exactly where we are. Through intentional practices of self-care, spiritual nurturing, and community support, we can move from simply surviving past hurts to thriving in the wholeness God intends for us.

Rewriting Your Relationship Narrative: Finding Purpose in Past Pain

The journey of redefining our past relationship experiences begins with a profound truth—every painful chapter can become a testimony of God's redemptive love and transformative power. Like precious metals refined by fire, our relationship histories don't have to remain sources of regret but can be transformed into wisdom that shapes a more purposeful future.

As Lane Moore beautifully articulates, "You already survived everything you survived, so offer yourself a day where you allow yourself to stay present." This gentle reminder aligns perfectly with Romans 8:28, which assures us that God works all things—even our painful experiences—together for good. The key lies not in trying to forget or minimize past hurts, but in allowing God to reshape our understanding of these experiences.

The process of rewriting our relationship narrative involves three essential elements that work together to create lasting transformation.[48]

First, we must practice acceptance without judgment—acknowledging our experiences and emotions without condemning ourselves or others. Second, we need to intentionally extract wisdom from each chapter of our relationships, asking ourselves what these experiences have taught us about ourselves, others, and God's faithfulness. Finally, we must integrate these insights into a new, empowering narrative that aligns with God's truth rather than our past pain.

Approaching this transformation through self-compassion proves invaluable, as John Kim emphasizes in his work on intentional singleness. Rather than viewing past relationships as failures or wasted time, we can choose to see them as vital chapters in our growth story. This perspective shift allows us to recognize how God has used each experience—even the painful ones—to shape us into who we are today.

Practical steps in this journey might include

- Journaling about past relationships from a perspective of learning rather than regret
- Identifying specific growth areas that emerged from each experience
- Practicing self-compassion through biblical affirmations.
- It's also helpful to share our evolving narrative with trusted friends or mentors who can offer wisdom and perspective while affirming God's ongoing work in our lives.

As we engage in this process, it's crucial to remember that rewriting our narrative isn't about denying pain or pretending hurt didn't happen. Instead, it's about allowing God to redeem our experiences and transform them into sources of wisdom and ministry to others. Consider how Joseph's perspective on his painful past evolved to recognize God's greater purpose: "You intended to harm me, but God intended it for good."

The way we interpret our past significantly impacts our present and future. Isaiah 43:18-19 encourages us: "Forget the former things; do not dwell on the past. See, I am doing a new thing!" This scripture doesn't call us to deny our history but invites us to view it through the lens of God's redemptive purpose rather than through the filter of pain or regret.

As you begin rewriting your own relationship narrative, remember that God's perspective on your story is one of hope and purpose. Let His truth guide your reflection and allow His love to heal the places where past relationships have left scars. Through this process, you'll discover that every chapter—even the painful ones—can be transformed into stepping stones toward a more purposeful and fulfilling future.

Building Healthy Boundaries: Protecting Your Heart While Remaining Open

Like delicate garden gates that both protect and welcome, healthy boundaries serve as sacred thresholds in our relationships—guarding our hearts while allowing authentic connection to flourish. The wisdom found in Proverbs 4:23 captures this beautifully: "Above all else, guard your heart, for everything you do flows from it." This divine guidance reminds us that boundaries aren't walls meant to isolate, but rather God-given guidelines enabling us to engage meaningfully while maintaining our emotional and spiritual well-being.

Many singles struggle with guilt when setting boundaries, fearing they might appear unfriendly or unspiritual. Yet understanding that boundaries are essential for self-care and spiritual growth helps alleviate this guilt.[49] As John Van Epp emphasizes, "Boundaries are great principles for people, regardless of their relationship status!" These boundaries help us honor both ourselves and others, creating space for genuine connection while preventing emotional exhaustion.

Jesus himself modeled healthy boundary-setting by regularly withdrawing from crowds to pray (Luke 5:16) and being selective about sharing certain truths (Matthew 7:6). His example shows us that boundaries aren't unspiritual—they're essential for maintaining our relationship with God and others. When we establish clear limits with grace and wisdom, we create sacred spaces where authentic relationships can flourish.

The journey of setting healthy boundaries often begins with honest self-reflection. What are your non-negotiables? Where have past boundary violations left you vulnerable? Emily Stimpson notes, "Living the life God wants us to live today is key to having a happy, holy marriage tomorrow and a happy, holy life always." This perspective highlights how boundaries aren't merely defensive mechanisms but proactive choices rooted in self-respect, faith, and purpose.

Practical steps for establishing healthy boundaries include defining your values clearly, communicating limits respectfully, and allowing others to earn trust gradually. Regular self-assessment of emotional energy, consistent prayer, and seeking counsel from trusted mentors help maintain these boundaries effectively. Healthy limits aren't rigid—they're flexible enough to adapt as you grow and heal.

As you implement boundaries, pay attention to both external pressures and internal resistance. Are you struggling to say 'no' out of fear of rejection? Are cultural or family expectations making it difficult to maintain your limits? These challenges are normal parts of the boundary-setting process. The key is responding with grace—both toward yourself and others—while remaining firm in your convictions.

Establishing boundaries also means developing discernment about whom to trust and how quickly to open up. Like a garden that needs both sunlight and protection, your heart requires both openness to genuine connection and safeguards against harm. This balance allows you to remain receptive to authentic relationships while honoring your need for emotional safety.

Remember that healthy boundaries actually enhance rather than inhibit genuine connection. When people know where you stand and what you value, it creates clarity and respect in relationships. As you grow in setting and maintaining boundaries, you'll likely find that your relationships become more authentic, your energy more focused, and your heart better protected while remaining beautifully open to God's best for your life.

As we conclude this chapter on healing and hope, let us remember that our journey of processing past relationships is both deeply personal and profoundly transformative. Like Ruby's story illustrates, the path from hurt to wholeness isn't just about moving past pain—it's about allowing God to redeem every experience for His greater purpose.

Through this chapter, we've explored how God's healing grace can transform our deepest wounds into wisdom and our painful experiences into platforms for ministry. We've learned that establishing healthy boundaries isn't about building walls but creating sacred spaces where authentic relationships can flourish. We've discovered that our past relationships, while significant chapters in our story, don't define our future.

Action Steps:

- Write a "Goodbye Letter." Write a letter to a past hurt or relationship. You don't have to send it. The purpose is to articulate your feelings, acknowledge the pain, and declare your choice to move forward in freedom.
- Identify One Lesson. Name one specific, valuable lesson you learned from a past difficult relationship that has made you wiser or stronger today.
- Create a "Hope" Playlist. Compile a list of worship songs that remind you of God's faithfulness, His healing power, and His promises for your future.

Key Chapter Takeaway:

- Every emotional wound can become a wellspring of wisdom when surrendered to God.
- Healing is both a journey and a destination, requiring patience and grace.
- Healthy boundaries protect your heart while allowing authentic connection.
- Your story is still being written, with the Master Author holding the pen.

The transformation we've witnessed through Ruby's story—from carrying the weight of past hurt to discovering purpose in her pain—reminds us that healing is possible when we surrender our hearts to God's restorative work. As she discovered, journaling, prayer, and authentic community become powerful tools in our healing journey.

Reflection Questions:

- How has God's grace been evident in your healing process?
- What limiting beliefs about past relationships need to be surrendered to God?
- In what ways can your story become a testimony of God's faithfulness?
- How have your boundaries evolved through this healing journey?

Scriptures for Meditation:

- Psalm 147:3—"He heals the brokenhearted and binds up their wounds."
- Isaiah 43:18-19—"Forget the former things; do not dwell on the past. See, I am doing a new thing!"
- 2 Corinthians 5:17—"Therefore, if anyone is in Christ, the new creation has come."

As you step forward from this chapter, carry with you the truth that healing isn't just about recovery—it's about discovery. It's about discovering God's faithfulness in every season, your resilience through every challenge, and the beautiful purpose He weaves through every experience.

Your past relationships don't diminish your worth or define your future. Instead, they become threads in the beautiful tapestry God is weaving in your life—a story of redemption, purpose, and grace.

May you walk forward with renewed hope, confident that the God who began this good work in you will be faithful to complete it. Your season of healing is not just about moving past pain—it's about stepping into the fullness of who God created you to be.

Prayer focus:

"Father, thank you for your healing grace that makes all things new. Help us to process our past with wisdom, embrace our present with courage, and step into our future with hope. May we trust You with both our wounds and our healing, knowing that You work all things together for our good. In Jesus' name, amen."

Chapter 10

Knowing Yourself in God: Building Your Inner Home

"And we know that in all things God works for the good of those who love Him."

In a world obsessed with titles—girlfriend, spouse, mother, entrepreneur—it's easy to build your identity on shifting circumstances. We often define ourselves by what we do, who we're connected to, or what others expect of us. But what happens when the job ends, the relationship changes, or expectations go unmet? If our identity rests there, it falls apart. This season of your life is a sacred invitation to begin a different kind of construction project. It's an opportunity to build your "inner home"—a place of self-knowledge and spiritual truth so solid that no storm can shake it. Before you can love well, lead well, or live well, you must first be at home with yourself in God.

Knowing yourself isn't just about discovering your passions or your personality type, though those are part of it. It's about becoming deeply rooted in the one identity that can never be taken away from you: you are God's beloved. This journey of self-knowledge is both liberating and rebellious in a world that would rather you find your identity somewhere else.

Laying the Foundation: Your Core Values

Every strong home begins with a solid foundation. For your inner home, that foundation is your core values. These are the non-negotiable principles that act as your internal compass, guiding your choices, defining your boundaries, and shaping your life.[50]

As a single person, you have an unparalleled opportunity to clarify these values without compromise. When you know what truly matters to you—things like integrity, compassion, creativity, or justice—you can align your life around them. Living outside of your core values creates a constant, low-grade internal conflict and anxiety. Living in alignment with them brings a profound sense of peace and rightness.

Take some time with a journal and ask yourself: What principles do I want my life to stand for? What matters most to me at the end of the day? This isn't about what you should value, but what you truly do value. This is the bedrock of your inner home.

Learning the Wiring: Your Emotional Patterns

Once the foundation is set, you need to understand the unique wiring of your home. Your emotions are not random reactions; they are signals from your soul, providing crucial information about your inner world. Learning to listen to them without judgment is a key part of self-awareness.

Perhaps you recognize some of these patterns: a surge of jealousy when a friend gets engaged, a wave of shame when a family member pressures you, or a deep sense of anxiety when your weekend is unstructured. Don't push these feelings away. Get curious about them. Each emotion has a story to tell. Ask yourself, "What is this feeling trying to tell me? What deeper belief or fear is it connected to?" When you learn to listen to your emotions, you can manage them instead of letting them manage you.

Decorating the Rooms with Grace: Embracing Your Story

Knowing yourself also means making peace with your own story. The rooms of our inner home are filled with memories—some beautiful, some painful. There are chapters in all of our lives that we wish we could tear out. But in God's economy, nothing is wasted. The parts of your story you wish had never happened are often the very places God wants to do His most redemptive work.

As Romans 8:28 reminds us, "And we know that in all things God works for the good of those who love Him." Your singleness, your childhood, your heartbreaks, your failures—none of it is beyond the reach of His redeeming hand.

This is a time to reclaim the parts of yourself that may have been silenced or set aside. Think about the dreams you dropped to please someone else, the passion you ignored because it didn't seem practical, or the playful, authentic parts of yourself you hid to fit in. Now is the time to invite those parts of you back home. Forgive yourself for the mistakes. Thank your younger self for getting you this far. Permit yourself to become again.

Seeing Yourself Through God's Eyes

Ultimately, building your inner home means seeing it—and yourself—the way your Creator does. To do that, you must immerse yourself in His truth. The Bible gives us a rich and stunning portrait of our true spiritual identity.

This means seeing yourself not through the distorted mirror of your last breakup, but through the clear lens of Scripture, which declares that you are chosen (Ephesians 1:4), deeply loved (Romans 5:8), and nothing less than God's masterpiece (Ephesians 2:10). It means knowing that you are fully redeemed (Ephesians 1:7) and complete in Christ (Colossians 2:10), right now. These are not just nice thoughts; they are foundational truths. When you believe them, you begin to live differently—with a quiet confidence, clear purpose, and a courageous heart.

This season is a sacred mirror. It's a time when you get to see yourself without the distraction of another person's reflection.[51] You'll see your beauty and your brokenness, your longings and your lies. And when you bring all of it before God, you give Him the space to lovingly furnish your inner home and make it a place of peace, strength, and wholeness.

The most powerful thing you can do in your singlehood is not to "find someone." It's to find yourself in God—to build your inner home on the rock of His truth and become so rooted in Him that when love comes, it finds you already whole.

Action steps:

- Get comfortable with the "Heart Check-In." Take a moment to question yourself, "What am I feeling right now, and why?" every day. Express these genuine feelings to God in prayer.
- Write down a brief vision statement. In one or two phrases, describe God's plan for you during this time. For instance, "Use my teaching gifts to mentor others."

- This week, make a list of your three basic principles and come up with one active method you can live out for each one.

Key Chapter Takeaway:

- Know the principles that drive your life
- Learn to listen to your emotions to manage them
- No moment of your life was a waste

Reflection Questions:

- What labels have I carried that are not from God?
- In what areas of my life do I struggle to believe that I am already complete?
- What are two or three of my non-negotiable core values?
- What parts of my personal story still need God's healing touch and my own acceptance?

Scripture to Meditate On:

- 1 Peter 2:9: "But you are a chosen people, a royal priesthood, a holy nation, God's special possession..."
- Ephesians 2:10: "For we are God's workmanship, created in Christ Jesus to do good works..."
- Psalm 139:23: "Search me, God, and know my heart; test me and know my anxious thoughts."
- Romans 8:28: "And we know that in all things God works for the good of those who love him..."

Prayer Focus:

Our Lord and Heavenly Father, thank you for my past, present, and future. I pray that you let me see the good in every process of my life with a heart of gratitude. And let me know and find myself in You in Jesus name, amen.

Chapter 11

Purpose Over Pressure: Living Beyond Expectations

"For the moment, all discipline seems painful rather than pleasant, but later it yields the peaceful fruit of righteousness to those who have been trained by it."

Singlehood often comes with an invisible soundtrack, a low, persistent hum of pressure. It's the ticking clock of expectations—from parents, from our church community, from social media, and loudest of all, from our own hearts. It's a voice that whispers, "You're behind," or "You're late," or "Something must be wrong with you."

But what if that pressure to measure up, to meet some imaginary timeline, is the very thing holding you back from the powerful, purpose-filled life God has for you right now? This chapter is about learning to tune out that noise and tune into a different frequency: the frequency of divine purpose.

Ben felt the pressure acutely. His best friend from college, Mark, had just sent a picture of his newborn son. Ben stared at the photo—the tiny, wrinkled face, the proud parents—and felt a complex mix of joy for his friend and a hollow ache for himself.

Mark was hitting all the life-script milestones: career, marriage, house, and now a baby. Meanwhile, Ben was still in his rented apartment, pouring his energy into his job and leading a youth group at his church. He loved his life, but in moments like this, it felt…lesser, stalled. The world was telling him he was falling behind.

That night, Ben opened his Bible to the story of Jeremiah. He read the familiar words, but this time they landed differently: "Before I formed you in the womb, I knew you; before you were born, I set you apart…" (Jeremiah 1:5). There was no mention of a wife, a mortgage, or a 401k. God's call on Jeremiah's life was direct, personal, and present. It wasn't contingent on anything or anyone else.

For Ben, this was a turning point. He began to see that the world puts pressure, but God gives purpose. And if your life doesn't look like everyone else's, it doesn't mean you've missed the mark. It might just mean you're walking the unique, narrow road God carved just for you.

Your Purpose Is Not Postponed

There is a pervasive and unbiblical lie that says your true purpose begins after you get married. That you need a partner to "complete your assignment." This is simply not true. God knew you and had a purpose for you before you were even a twinkle in your parents' eyes. Marriage is a beautiful calling for many, but it is not a prerequisite for impact. Your purpose is not postponed because you are single; you are already chosen, assigned, and called for such a time as this.[52]

Instead of asking God, "When will this season end?" Try asking a different question: "What is this season meant to build in me?"

Perhaps this season is God's invitation for you to finally write that book, to build a ministry from the ground up, or to pour yourself into mentoring someone who needs your wisdom. It might be the quiet space you need to heal from past wounds or the flexible time required to go back to school and pursue a lifelong dream. God does not waste our seasons; He refines us in them. When you embrace His design, you stop chasing timelines and start walking for a timeless purpose.

The Poison of Comparison

Nothing will kill your purpose faster than comparison. In this age of Instagram, every wedding announcement, tropical vacation, and baby picture can feel like a painful reminder of what you don't have. But God never asked you to run anyone's race but your own.

Hebrews 12:1-2 tells us to "run with perseverance the race marked out for us, fixing our eyes on Jesus." The moment you start looking over at someone else's lane, you lose momentum in your own. The next time you feel the sting of comparison, try this: first, thank God for the blessing He has given your friend. Celebrate with them genuinely. Then, immediately return your eyes to Jesus and ask, "Lord, what beautiful thing are You calling me to build in my lane today?" Comparison is a trap that makes you covet what is not yours; purpose is a calling that makes you steward what is.

When Purpose Feels Delayed

Sometimes the pressure comes not from comparison but from a sense of delay—especially if you've been faithful and still haven't seen the breakthrough you long for. It's easy to believe God is ignoring you or punishing you.

But in the Bible, delay is never denial. It is development.

Joseph waited in a prison cell for years, a forgotten man, before God elevated him to lead a nation.

David was anointed king as a teenager but spent decades running for his life in the wilderness before he ever sat on the throne.

God is not slow; He is strategic. If you are in a season of waiting, trust that He is using this time to prepare your character to be able to sustain your calling. Don't let the pressure of time push you into fear or a bad decision. Let the promise of His purpose pull you into deeper trust.

Living from Purpose, Not for Pressure

Your purpose isn't some grand, far-off destination. It's something God wants to reveal and release in your life right now. Ephesians 2:10 says we were created "for good works, which God prepared beforehand that we should walk in them." This means there are purpose-filled tasks assigned to you for this very day. You don't need to be married to be useful; you just need to be available.

When you begin to walk in purpose, you operate from a place of spiritual rest, not anxious striving. Pressure says, "Do more! Prove yourself! Keep up!" Purpose says, "Be still. Abide in His presence. Listen to His voice." It's from that place of abiding that you will bear much fruit (John 15:5).

Release the pressure. Embrace your purpose. You are chosen, assigned, and planted in this season for a reason.

Action Steps:

- Write your ideal "day in the life" five years from now.
- Design the small steps you can take now to bring it closer.

Key Chapter Takeaway:

- Don't put pressure on yourself because your life doesn't look like others'.
- God is strategic and not slow.
- Comparison is a trap that kills your purpose faster than you can imagine.

Reflection Questions:

- Whose expectations—my parents', my friends', or my own—am I trying to meet right now?
- Where in my life am I feeling the most pressure, and what is the source of that feeling?
- What has God placed in my hands to do in this specific season?
- How can I intentionally shift my focus from timelines to God's purpose for me today?

Scripture to Meditate On:

- Jeremiah 1:5: "Before I formed you in the womb, I knew you; before you were born, I set you apart..."
- Romans 12:2: "Do not conform to the pattern of this world, but be transformed by the renewing of your mind."
- Psalm 138:8: "The Lord will fulfill his purpose for me..."
- Isaiah 55:8-9: "For my thoughts are not your thoughts, neither are your ways my ways,' declares the Lord."

Prayer focus:

Thank you, my Lord and God, for what you are doing for my friends. Please, give me the heart to focus on you and your purpose and not on the pressures around me. As I navigate through life challenges, may I always remember to seek your guidance and strength and help me rest on your promises. Let my heart overflow with joy and peace, trusting that you are working all things together for good in Jesus' name, amen.

Chapter 12

Living Without Limits: Thriving in Your Single Season

"As a person thinks in their heart, so are they."

Just as a caterpillar must break out of its cocoon to become a butterfly, we must also break free from limiting beliefs that keep us from reaching our full potential. The journey from limitation to freedom begins when we realize that God's plan for our lives is much bigger than our current situation or relationship status. In the following pages, we'll explore how many of the "wise" or "careful" choices we make are actually excuses that hold us back from the abundant life Jesus promised in John 10:10. You'll see how self-doubt, delayed dreams, or the idea that "life will begin when I get married" can quietly trap us in a waiting season of our own making.

Take Poppy's story, for example. Like many singles, she built her life around what she thought was "appropriate" for someone unmarried—turning down travel opportunities, putting off school, and delaying buying a home. But through a mentoring session at church, God began to open her eyes and remove those self-imposed limits one by one. Her experience shows that our biggest obstacles are rarely external—they often come from within, shaped by what we believe is possible or "acceptable" for our single season.

This transformation mirrors the Apostle Paul's bold declaration from a prison cell: "I can do all things through Christ who strengthens me" (Philippians 4:13). His example challenges us to see beyond our current season and embrace the full scope of possibilities God has placed before us. Like Paul, we're called to live lives of impact and purpose, regardless of our circumstances or relationship status.

One of the most liberating truths we'll explore is that God's purpose for your life isn't on hold until marriage.[53] He's not waiting for a relationship status change to use you powerfully or bless you abundantly. As Scripture reminds us in Ephesians 2:10, "We are His workmanship, created in Christ Jesus for good works, which God prepared beforehand that we should walk in them." These good works—your purpose, calling, and impact—are available to you right now.

As we delve deeper into this chapter, we'll examine practical strategies for identifying and dismantling self-limiting beliefs, stepping into bold faith-filled living, and creating a legacy that transcends relationship status. You'll discover how to cultivate a mindset of abundance rather than scarcity and how to embrace opportunities for growth and impact that this unique season affords you.

Through biblical wisdom, practical exercises, and inspiring examples like Poppy's story of purchasing her home, completing her master's degree, and leading international ministry outreach, you'll discover how to move from merely surviving your single season to truly thriving in it. You'll learn to recognize and challenge the subtle ways you might be holding yourself back and develop the confidence to pursue God's best for your life—starting right where you are.

Prepare to be challenged, inspired, and equipped to break free from the invisible cage of limiting beliefs and step into the spacious place God has prepared for you. Your single season isn't a waiting room—it's a launchpad for living the extraordinary life God has designed for you. The only question is: are you ready to spread your wings and soar?

Breaking Free from Self-Limiting Beliefs: Embracing Your Full Potential

The invisible prison of self-limiting beliefs often holds us captive more effectively than any physical chains. As Proverbs 23:7 reminds us, "As a person thinks in their heart, so are they." These self-imposed limitations can be particularly binding during our single season, whispering lies about what we can achieve, who we can become, and what opportunities we should pursue.

Many singles find themselves unconsciously adopting beliefs that constrain their potential—"I'll start that business after marriage," "I can't buy a house until I have a partner," or "My life won't really begin until I find the right person."[54] These thoughts, though seemingly protective, actually become barriers that keep us from experiencing the abundant life Jesus promised in John 10:10.

God's perspective of our potential isn't limited by our relationship status. Ephesians 3:20 declares that He "can do exceedingly abundantly above all that we ask or think." This truth invites us to expand our vision and embrace the full scope of possibilities before us. Just as the Israelites had to shift their mindset from slavery to freedom after leaving Egypt, we too must transform our thinking patterns.

The journey to breaking free begins with identifying these limiting beliefs that have taken root in our hearts. Through my years of mentoring singles, I've witnessed how these invisible barriers manifest in various ways—postponed dreams, scaled-down ambitions, and lives lived in a perpetual holding pattern. But I've also seen the extraordinary transformation that occurs when these barriers are confronted with God's truth.

Sarah was a gifted architect who had convinced herself that pursuing her dream of starting her own firm would have to wait until marriage. Through prayer and mentorship, she began to challenge this belief, eventually launching her practice and securing several major contracts. Her testimony reminds us that our capacity for impact and success isn't tied to our relationship status but to our willingness to trust God's timing and purpose.

Breaking free requires both spiritual renewal and practical action. The apostle Paul encourages us in Romans 12:2 to "be transformed by the renewing of your mind." This transformation involves:

- Identifying limiting beliefs through regular self-reflection and prayer
- Challenging these beliefs with Scripture and God's promises
- Taking bold steps of faith, even when they feel uncomfortable
- Celebrating progress and learning from setbacks

- Building a support system of faith-filled believers who champion your growth

As you begin this journey of transformation, remember that 2 Timothy 1:7 declares, "God has not given us a spirit of fear, but of power and of love and of a sound mind." This truth empowers us to step into our full potential without waiting for circumstances to change.

Your single season serves as a starting point for the remarkable life that God intended for you. Every day presents opportunities to challenge old limitations and embrace new possibilities. Whether it's pursuing further education, starting a ministry, buying property, or launching a business, God's timing for your dreams isn't necessarily tied to your relationship status.

Going forward, I encourage you to take inventory of the limiting beliefs that may be holding you back.

What dreams have you postponed?

What opportunities have you declined?

What aspects of your life are you putting on hold?

Now is the time to bring these beliefs into the light of God's truth and begin taking steps toward the abundant life He has promised. Your potential isn't determined by your status but by your willingness to embrace God's vision for your life. As you break free from self-limiting beliefs, you'll discover that this season of singleness can be one of unprecedented growth, impact, and fulfillment.

Creating a Legacy: Making an Impact Beyond Relationship Status

Your legacy isn't measured by relationship status but by the divine purpose you fulfill and the lives you touch. As singles, we have a unique opportunity to shape an impact that reaches far beyond conventional expectations, touching the very heart of God's purpose for our lives. The Apostle Paul, writing in 1 Corinthians 7:32-34, illuminates this truth, highlighting how the unmarried person can be singularly focused on the Lord's affairs; a powerful reminder that our legacy potential is amplified, not diminished, by our single status.

God's perspective on legacy extends far beyond traditional definitions. Throughout Scripture, we see remarkable examples of individuals whose impact wasn't defined by their marital status but by their unwavering obedience to God's calling. Daniel, who influenced kingdoms, or Mary of Bethany, whose act of worship Jesus declared would be remembered wherever the gospel is preached (Matthew 26:13). Their stories remind us that lasting impact flows from alignment with divine purpose, not relationship status.

As a single person, you possess unique advantages for legacy-building that married individuals might not have. Your flexibility, focused energy, and undivided attention create unprecedented opportunities for impact. Whether through mentoring others, launching ministry initiatives, or pursuing career excellence that glorifies God, your single season offers distinct possibilities for creating ripple effects that will continue long after you're gone.

Maya was a software engineer who initially viewed her singleness as a limitation. Through prayer and mindset transformation, she recognized her season as an opportunity for unique impact. She began mentoring young women in STEM fields, eventually founding a nonprofit that provides coding education to underprivileged girls. Her legacy now extends far beyond what she initially imagined possible, touching hundreds of lives and inspiring future generations.

Building a meaningful legacy requires intentional action and divine perspective. Here are key principles for legacy-building in your single season:

- Identify your sphere of influence and unique gifting
- Invest deeply in others' growth and development
- Create sustainable initiatives that will outlive you
- Document your journey and lessons learned.
- Build meaningful connections and mentor relationships.

Your impact isn't limited by your status but expanded by your availability to God's purposes. Psalm 145:4 reminds us that *"One generation shall praise Your works to another, and shall declare Your mighty acts."* Your single season provides unique opportunities to sow seeds of impact that will bear fruit for generations to come.

As we conclude this transformative journey through thriving in singleness, let this truth settle deeply in your heart: your legacy isn't about what you accumulate but about what you contribute. Every day presents new opportunities to invest in others, share wisdom, and create lasting impact. The question isn't whether you'll leave a legacy—you will. The question is what kind of legacy you'll choose to build.

Single season isn't a waiting room for legacy-building—it's your divine appointment for maximum impact. Embrace it with courage, purpose, and unwavering faith in the God who has called you to such a time as this. Let your life become a testament to His faithfulness and a beacon of hope for generations to come.

Taking Bold Steps: Practical Strategies for Pursuing Your Purpose

The journey from vision to reality requires more than good intentions—it demands bold, decisive action rooted in faith and purpose. Like a seed breaking through soil to reach sunlight, pursuing your divine purpose often means pushing through comfort zones and familiar territories. As Hebrews 11:1 reminds us, *"Faith is the substance of things hoped for, the evidence of things not seen."* This faith, combined with practical wisdom and strategic action, forms the foundation for pursuing your God-given purpose with boldness and intention.

Bold steps begin with radical acceptance of your present season while taking intentional steps toward your calling. This aligns perfectly with Paul's teaching in Philippians 3:13-14 about *"pressing toward the mark for the prize of the high calling of God in Christ Jesus."* Your purpose isn't waiting for a relationship status change—it's calling you to action today!

Consider these practical strategies for taking bold steps toward your purpose:

- Start with Divine Connection
- Develop consistent prayer and meditation practices
- Create space for hearing God's voice
- Study Scripture related to your calling
- Journal divine insights and promptings

Build Strategic Foundations

- Set clear, purpose-driven goals
- Create accountability structures
- Develop necessary skills and knowledge
- Establish healthy routines and habits

Take Intentional Action

- Start with small, consistent steps
- Challenge comfort zones regularly
- Learn from setbacks and adjust course
- Celebrate progress and victories
- Breaking free from self-limiting beliefs
- Creating a legacy beyond relationship status
- Taking bold steps in pursuing purpose

Action Steps:

- Dismantle One Lie. Identify one self-limiting belief (e.g., "I can't buy a house alone"). Spend 15 minutes researching or brainstorming all the reasons that the belief isn't true.
- Take One Bold Step. Choose one small but courageous action from your brainstorming and do it this week (e.g., contact a realtor for information, sign up for the class, write the first page of the business plan).
- Start Your Legacy Project. Identify one person you can intentionally invest in or one cause you can consistently support with your time or talent, starting this month.

Key Chapter Takeaway:

- Your life can serve as an expression of God's faithfulness and a source of hope for future generations.
- Taking the path from vision to reality necessitates bold, action-oriented initiatives founded in faith and commitment.
- It is not only about you surviving the season, but also about thriving and flourishing above the survival mode and acknowledging the abundance that is encompassed in your life.

Reflection Questions:

- What limiting beliefs am I ready to release?
- How can I start building my legacy today?
- What bold step is God calling me to take?
- Where do I need to expand my vision of what's possible?
- What does the word "legacy" mean to me? What kind of legacy am I building with my choices today?

Scriptures For Meditation:

- Philippians 4:13 - "I can do all things through Christ who strengthens me"
- Joshua 1:9 - "Have I not commanded you? Be strong and courageous"
- Ephesians 3:20 - "Now to Him who can do exceedingly abundantly above all that we ask or think"

Prayer Focus:

My Lord and God, thank you for your plans and purpose for my life. Today, I choose to live without self-imposed limits, embracing the extraordinary life You have designed for me. Please, help me to build a legacy that brings glory to your name, because in Christ, all things are possible, and I step forward in faith to fulfill Your calling on my life, in Jesus' name, Amen.

Conclusion

As we draw this journey to a close, I'm reminded of the profound truth that has anchored every chapter of this book: your season of singleness is not a waiting period but a divine appointment for transformation, purpose, and extraordinary impact.

Throughout this book, we've learned that being single isn't something to merely get through. It's a special time to discover who you are, strengthen your relationship with God, and prepare for all that He has planned for you. Together, we've explored how to live with purpose, set healthy boundaries, manage your life wisely, and build meaningful relationships—all while staying grounded in Jesus Christ. You now have both practical tools and spiritual insight to live whole and fulfilled. But above all, remember this: your completeness is found in Christ alone—not in your relationship status or life situation. As you move forward, keep these truths close to your heart:

- Your worth is eternally established in Christ, independent of your relationship status.
- Every season holds divine purpose and opportunities for impact.
- Your single season is a gift to be stewarded with wisdom and intentionality.
- Building a purposeful life begins now, not when your circumstances change.

Scriptures to Anchor Your Heart:

- *"For I know the thoughts that I think toward you," says the LORD, "thoughts of peace and not of evil, to give you a future and a hope."—Jeremiah 29:11*
- *"Being confident of this very thing, that He who has begun a good work in you will complete it until the day of Jesus Christ."—Philippians 1:6*

Questions for Continued Growth:

- How has your perspective on singleness evolved through this journey?
- What specific steps will you take to embrace your purpose in this season?
- How can you use your current season to create lasting impact in the lives of others?

Your story is still unfolding. This is not your rush season; it's a vital part of your walk with God. Embrace it confidently, live it purposefully, and trust that God is using every moment for your growth and His glory. Walk forward with renewed vision and faith. You are complete in Christ, equipped for every good work, and positioned for impact right where you are.

Go boldly, knowing that you already have everything you need to live a life filled with passion, purpose, and joy. The world needs your light, your voice, and your faithfulness in this very season.

Your single season isn't about waiting; it's about becoming. Embrace it fully, live it with purpose, and watch God transform your life in ways beyond your imagination.

Acknowledgement

First and foremost, I return all glory, honor, and praise to God Almighty—the Author of life and the Giver of purpose. Without His wisdom, guidance, and unfailing love, this book would not have been conceived or completed. Every page of *Living Whole* is a testimony of His grace and a reminder that we are complete in Him.

To the Holy Spirit, my Teacher and ever-present Help, thank You for inspiring every thought, whispering truth to my heart, and strengthening me through this journey.

To my family and loved ones, whose love and prayers gave me courage—you are my earthly blessings.

To my entire team – your thoughtful critiques, incisive questions, and unwavering commitment to refining this message have made this book so much stronger. Thank you for your hard work in bringing these words to the world.

To every single person whose story, struggles, and triumphs inspired this book—this is for you. You are not forgotten, overlooked, or incomplete. You are whole in Christ, and your journey matters.

Finally, to every reader holding this book, thank you for allowing me into your life. My prayer is that these words ignite faith, restore joy, and empower you to embrace singlehood with power, passion, and purpose.

With a grateful heart, I say - thank you.

About the Author

The author is deeply committed to mentoring and coaching people through the diverse seasons of life, helping them discover their purpose, cultivate self-awareness, and walk in wholeness. Compelled by compassion and guided by faith, she serves with a deep conviction that every life is valuable, and every season holds divine purpose.

With a heart for personal growth and spiritual clarity, she empowers individuals to align with their God-given purpose and develop into the best version of themselves in Christ. Her message is clear and compelling: embrace every season with intentionality, steward each day with wisdom, and pursue a life of meaning rooted in divine purpose.

She believes that every phase of life holds significance and offers opportunities for transformation. Through her work, she helps others create lives of passion, authenticity, and fulfilment—not defined by external validation, but by inner completeness.

REFERENCE

Chapter 1

[1] Kim, J. (2021). *Single On Purpose: Redefine Everything. Find Yourself First.* SoBrief. https://sobrief.com/books/single-on-purpose

[2] Kim, J. (2020, December 22). *Single on Purpose.* Barnes & Noble.

[3] Slawson, N. (2025, February 11). *Single: Living a Complete Life on Your Own Terms.* Goodreads. https://www.goodreads.com/en/book/show/213243924-single

Chapter 2

[4] DePaulo, B. (2019, March 11). *Here Are My Reviews and Discussions of Books about Single Life.* Bella DePaulo. https://belladepaulo.com/2019/03/here-are-my-reviews-and-discussions-of-books-about-single-life/

[5] Smith, A. & Dallas, B. S. (2012, August 1). *Singlehood Redefined.* Goodreads. https://www.goodreads.com/book/show/15736914-singlehood-redefined

[6] Shackelford S. & Perea A. (2018, October 29). *Myth Busting: Myths About Being Single.* PCA-NWA. https://pca-nwa.com/myth-busting-myths-about-being-single/

[7] Estrada, A. (2006, December 13). *UCSB Social Psychologist Debunks Myths of Singles and Singlehood.* UC Santa Barbara News. https://news.ucsb.edu/2006/012199/ucsb-social-psychologist-debunks-myths-singles-and-singlehood

[8] White, S. (2019, September 4). *"7 Myths About Singleness" by Sam Allberry.* Modern Reformation.

https://www.modernreformation.org/resources/articles/the-mod-7-myths-about-singleness-by-sam-allberry

[9] Piper J. (2019, January 17). *5 Myths about Singleness*. Crossway. https://www.crossway.org/articles/5-myths-about-singleness/

[10] Leutwiler Campbell, C. (2012, July 01). *Singleness Redefined: Living Life to the Fullest*. The Gospel Coalition Store. https://store.thegospelcoalition.org/product/9781596381117/singleness-redefined-paperback

Chapter 3

[11] Workplace Strategies for Mental Health. (2021, January 29). *Emotional intelligence self-assessment*. Workplace Strategies for Mental Health. https://www.workplacestrategiesformentalhealth.com/resources/emotional-intelligence-self-assessment

[12] Bibilamour. (2020, October). *What Does It Mean To Be Complete In Christ*. Bibilamour04.com. https://www.bibilamour04.com/2020/10/what-does-it-mean-to-be-complete-in.html

[13] Lowe, T. (2025, August 1) *10 Self-Awareness Examples for Personal Growth (FREE Tool)*. Loving Life Co. https://lovinglifeco.com/personal-growth/10-self-awareness-examples-for-personal-growth/

[14] Edmundson, M. (2025, April 27). *What We Learned About Biblical Wholeness And Where We Go Next*. CROWD Church. https://crowd.church/talks/what-we-learned-about-biblical-wholeness-and-where-we-go-next

[15] Wallbridge A. (2023, February 27). *The Importance Of Self-Awareness In Emotional Intelligence*. TSW Training.

https://www.tsw.co.uk/blog/leadership-and-management/self-awareness-in-emotional-intelligence/

[16] Management Concepts. (2023, October 15). *How Emotional Intelligence Helps Your Professional Growth*. Management Concepts. https://www.managementconcepts.com/resource/how-emotional-intelligence-helps-your-professional-growth/

[17] Ndungu, W. (2023, July 4). *6 Books On Being Happily Single*. Hooting Owl. https://hootingowl.co/6-books-on-being-happily-single/

[18] Faith and Health Connection. (2023). *Wholeness - A Biblical and Christian Perspective*. Faith and Health Connection. https://www.faithandhealthconnection.org/the_connection/spirit-soul-and-body/wholeness-biblical-and-christian-perspective/

Chapter 4

[19] Dittman, M. R. (2020, September 10). *How Being Single Makes You Complete - Part 1*. Mary Dittman. https://marydittman.mykajabi.com/blog/how-being-single-makes-you-complete-part-1

[20] Sng P. H. (2022, March 10). *The Sacred Place of Solitude*. Cornerstone Community Church. https://www.cscc.org.sg/weekly-blog/the-sacred-place-of-solitude/

[21] Joseph, E. L. S. (2023, September 27). *Solitude and the Contemplative Life*. Redbud Writers Guild. https://redbudwritersguild.com/solitude-and-the-contemplative-life/

[22] Paiva, A. (2023, October 1). *Embracing Solitude, Overcoming Loneliness: A Christian and Psychological Perspective*. Cumberland Centers. https://cumberlandcenters.org/blog/embracing-solitude-overcoming-loneliness-a-christian-and-psychological-perspective

[23] Barton, R. H. (2015, August). *Solitude: In God for the World*. Transforming Center. https://transformingcenter.org/2015/08/solitude-sake-others/

[24] Outdoor Apothecary. (2023, October). *Creating a Sacred Space: A Guide to Finding Peace and Harmony*. The Outdoor Apothecary. https://www.outdoorapothecary.com/sacred-space/

[25] Aman, J. (2024). *How to Create a Sacred Space at Home for Prayer & Meditation*. JodiAman.com. https://jodiaman.com/blog/sacred-space/

[26] Mansfield, Elaine. (2016, September 13). *10 Ways to Create Sacred Space Every Day*. Elaine Mansfield. https://elainemansfield.com/2016/10-ways-create-sacred-space-every-day/

[27] Hatmaker, J. (2025, April 2). *4 Simple Steps to Create Sacred Spaces in a Busy Home*. Jen Hatmaker. https://jenhatmaker.com/blog/4-simple-steps-to-create-sacred-spaces-in-a-busy-home/

[28] Jean. (2017, January 19). *How to Create Inner Sacred Space*. Healthy Spirituality. https://healthyspirituality.org/create-inner-sacred-space/

Chapter 5

[29] DePaulo, B. (2019, June 22). *Single Life in the 21st Century: A Guide to Owning It*. Psychology Today. https://www.psychologytoday.com/us/blog/living-single/201906/single-life-in-the-21st-century-a-guide-to-owning-it

[30] Breen, P. (2020, January 22). *3 Must-Read Online Dating Books for Catholic Singles*. Catholic Singles. https://www.catholicsingles.com/blog/online-dating-books/

[31] Walmart Stores, Inc. (2025). *Robot or human?*. Walmart.com. https://www.walmart.com/ip/Singleness-Redefined-Living-Life-to-the-Fullest-Paperback-9781596381117/180929407

Chapter 6

[32] Kim, J. (2021, December 28). *Single On Purpose: Redefine Everything. Find Yourself First.*. Auntie's Bookstore.

https://auntiesbooks.com/book/9780062980748

[33] Widder, W. (2000, May 23). *Living Whole Without a Better Half: Biblical Truth for the Single Life*. Goodreads.

https://www.goodreads.com/book/show/18637323-living-whole-without-a-better-half

[34] Lumia. (2023, August 10). *10 Self Awareness Tools For Coaches*. Lumia Coaching. https://www.lumiacoaching.com/blog/self-awareness-tools

Chapter 7

[35] CSN. (2023, June 22). *Biblical Financial Principles and 5 Practical Steps to Live by Them*. Christian Stewardship Network. https://www.christianstewardshipnetwork.com/blog/2023/6/22/biblical-financial-principles-and-5-practical-steps-to-live-by-them

[36] Bennett, R. L. (2024, March 05). *Financial Fireworks: 7 Strategies to Help You Build Financial Independence*. TCDRS. https://www.tcdrs.org/library/7-strategies-for-financial-independence/

[37] Douglas. (2025, January 21). *Biblical Financial Stewardship: Principles, Practices, and Living a Faithful Money Management Life*. Franklin Wealth Management. https://www.franklin-wealth.com/resources/biblical-financial-stewardship/

[38] Helmer, B. (2020, February 13). *5 Financial Planning Tips for Singles*. Wealth Enhancement. https://www.wealthenhancement.com/blog/financial-planning-tips-for-singles

[39] PLACE. (2023, November 30). *Achieving Financial Freedom: Steps to Build Wealth and Live the Life You Want*. PLACE. https://place.com/real-estate-business/achieving-financial-freedom-steps-to-build-wealth/

[40] Town & Country Federal Credit Union. (2024, July 17). *10 Smart Money Moves for Single People*. Town & Country Federal Credit Union. https://www.tcfcu.com/budget/10-smart-money-moves-for-single-people/

[41] MyBudgetCoach. (2025, March 31). *Solo Financial Freedom: Top Tips for Singles Financial Planning*. MyBudgetCoach. https://www.mybudgetcoach.com/blog/solo-financial-freedom-top-tips-for-singles-financial-planning

[42] The Bonhoeffer Project. (2023, April). *The Disciple and Money: A Lesson in Stewardship*. Discipleship.org. https://discipleship.org/blog/the-disciple-and-money-a-lesson-in-stewardship/

[43] INJOY Stewardship Solutions. (2025, February). *3 Biblical Principles for Managing Personal Finances*. INJOY Stewardship. https://injoystewardship.com/3-biblical-principles-for-managing-personal-finances/

Chapter 8

[44] American Red Cross. (2023, December 31). *Disaster Preparedness Plan*. American Red Cross. https://www.redcross.org/get-help/how-to-prepare-for-emergencies/make-a-plan.html

[45] Tomlin, K. (2024, January 15). *Intentional Singleness*. Heart of Dating. https://www.heartofdating.com/podcast/intentional-singleness

[46] Olaleye, T. (2023). *Single and Whole: Living Life to the Full Before You Meet the Right Person*. Walmart.com. https://www.walmart.com/ip/Single-and-Whole-Living-Life-to-the-Full-Before-You-Meet-the-Right-Person-Paperback-9781908588340/383727598

Chapter 9

[47] Washington State Department of Health. (2023, September 1). *Get Ready for an Emergency*. Washington State Department of Health. https://doh.wa.gov/emergencies/be-prepared-be-safe/get-ready

[48] Kislev, E. (2019, February). *Happy Singlehood: The Rising Acceptance and Celebration of Solo Living*. University of California Press. https://www.ucpress.edu/books/happy-singlehood/paper

[49] Simon, T. (2024, January 15). *Being Single: An Intentional Experiment*. Sounds True. https://resources.soundstrue.com/transcript/being-single-an-intentional-experiment/

Chapter 10

[50] Sarkhedi, B. (2025, April 24). *Seven Books About Being Single and Happy in 2025*. Unproposed. https://unproposed.com/seven-books-about-being-single-and-happy/

[51] Stimpson, E. (2012, February). *Emily Stimpson: The Catholic Girl's Guide to Being Single*. CatholicMatch Plus. https://plus.catholicmatch.com/articles/emily-stimpson-we-single-catholics-are-a-new-reality

Chapter 11

[52] Evans, T. (2018, August 1). *Kingdom Single: Living Complete and Fully Free*. Goodreads. https://goodreads.com/book/show/39920930.KingdomSingleLivingCompleteandFullyFree

Chapter 12

[53] Josephine. (2016, February 11). *Relishing the Single Life in a Couple's World*. thoughts and afterthoughts. https://thoughtsandafterthoughts.com/2016/02/11/relishing-the-single-life-in-a-couples-world/

[54] Schneider, H. (2019, March 22). *8 Eye-Opening Books To Read If You're Learning To Love Being Single*. Elite Daily. https://www.elitedaily.com/p/8-books-to-read-when-youre-single-that-will-change-your-perspective-16902172

www.ingramcontent.com/pod-product-compliance
Lightning Source LLC
LaVergne TN
LVHW051603070426
835507LV00021B/2739